Joy in the Seasons of Life:

Walking Each Other Home to God

James McReynolds
Minister of Joy to the World

Joy in the Seasons of Life: Walking Each Other Home to God
ISBN: Softcover 978-1-955581-18-9
Copyright © 2021 by James McReynolds

All rights reserved. No part of this book may be reproduced or transmitted in any form or by any means, electronic or mechanical, including photocopying, recording, or by any information storage and retrieval system, without permission in writing from the publisher.

Parson's Porch Books is an imprint of Parson's Porch & Company (PP&C) in Cleveland, Tennessee. PP&C is an innovative organization which raises money by publishing books of noted authors, representing all genres. Its face and voice is **David Russell Tullock** (dtullock@parsonsporch.com).

Parson's Porch & Company *turns books into bread & milk* by sharing its profits with the poor.

www.parsonsporch.com

Joy in the Seasons of Life

Other Books by James McReynolds Published by Parson's Porch Books

The Spirituality of Joy: The Least Discussed Human Emotion

The Joy of Preaching: Encountering Jesus through the Word of God

Dancing with God: A Theology of Joy

The Silence of the Church: The Spiritual Struggle with Sexuality

The Spirit of Joy Church

Joy Comes in the Mourning: Love Is Forever

The Joy of Prayer:
The Way to Intimacy with God Envisioning the Great Commission:

The Joy of the Kingdom Walking in the Garden with God:
Journey to Jouissance

Joy in the Seasons of Life:
Walking Each Other Home to God

Dedication

To my outstanding bonus sons and grandsons:

Scott Anderson

Bryan Baker

Rick Richardson

Bill Raskind

Bonus Grandsons:

Alex Baker

Ethan Coffin

John McReynolds

Joseph McReynolds

Contents

Dedication 6

Foreword 10

Preface 15

Introduction to Joy 30

Spring 53

Summer 91

Fall 105

Winter 129

Bibliography 163

Acknowledgements 171

About the Author 173

Foreword

I don't think I have ever known anyone who experiences joy the way James McReynolds does.

Jim is my friend. I have known him many years. He seems to breathe joy in the way most of us inhale the air around us, naturally and continually. And the best thing is that he writes about it.

Jim lets us in on the sources and products of the joy in our lives all the time. He writes with a lightness and beauty we would not otherwise know. He permits us to experience some of the rarefied enjoyment that he himself actually lives with all the time.

It is wonderful that Jim has written a book about the seasons of joy in our lives—how joys morph and reemerge in new forms throughout our lifetimes, and how paying attention to these joys can enrich and bless the human psyche at every stage.

Jim has peppered his chapters with stories and illustrations that will charm, enrich, and truly enlighten his readers. This is the gift God has given him. The very concept he is working with, talking about the joys of life in the various seasons of our lives, has already caused me to think about the multiple joys in the seasons of my own life.

I recall my general happiness in childhood, the springtime of my life, and how wonderful it was to grow up in a quiet, lovely neighborhood in a small town and have my early schooling under some wonderful, kindhearted teachers. In those early years, when the weather was good, I especially loved playing for hours at a time under a big, overarching bush outside our house and pretending a lot of things that I know helped to deepen and enrich my whole life.

Then came the delights of going to college, making new friends, and finding my way into the work of the Christian ministry. I recall with pleasure the small country churches I served during my summer years, and the simple, warm-hearted goodness of the farmers and laborers who attended those churches. The joys of those little churches eventually gave way to a whole new set of joys as I pastored other, larger congregations, and as I do sometimes, left my ministerial job for a few years to teach in a college or a university. It was while I was teaching at Vanderbilt University Divinity School in Nashville, in fact, that I first encountered young James McReynolds, then an employee of the Sunday School Board. I enjoyed his friendship both inside the classroom and in the halls and extracurricular life of the university.

What were the special joys of my autumn years? At this point, I was being given incredible opportunities to travel abroad, offering seminars to Air Force chaplains in other parts of the world, and my growing family often enjoyed the benefits of journeying with me. I also had the pleasure of publishing a number of books about a lot of things that I hoped mattered to other people as much as they did to me.

Now I am in the winter of my life, and, wonder of wonders, the joys still abound. My greatest joys are the active exchanges I continue to have with former students, parishioners, and professional acquaintances—people like Jim. I am grateful for the Internet, and the ease which I can communicate with all these wonderful folks. I approach my computer eagerly each morning, looking forward to seeing who has written since the day before. I am grateful to share in many friends' lives not only all over the United States, but on foreign shores as well.

I am sure, from what I have already read in *Joy in the Seasons of Life: Walking Each Other Home to God*, this beautifully written book will remind us of joys we haven't thought about.

It reinforces us in remembering the joys of which we are already aware. Every reader will owe a great debt of thankfulness to its extraordinary percipient author for enriching our lives—again. Jim is truly, as the renowned Norman Vincent Peale called him, God's Minister of Joy to the World that always needs to be made more aware of the many things that continually enrich and beautify our lives.

Dr. John Killinger | Warrenton, Virginia

Joy in the Seasons of Life

Joy IS *A CHOICE*

"You and I were created for joy, and if we miss it, we miss The reason for existence. If our joy is honest joy, it must somehow be congruous with human tragedy. This is the test of joy's integrity. Is joy compatible with pain? Only the heart that hurts has a right to joy."

--Lewis Smedes

Preface

Definitions of joy that psychologists use conflicts with each other. My books on joy aim toward stimulation of more research on joy. Being surrounded by joyful people potentiates joy. Joy increases as we share it. Rejoicing increases the joy of each. Beginning in studies at Vanderbilt, I have spent 50 years focusing on joy. My last formal study was at Yale Divinity School in the Theology of Joy and the Good Life project. Joy is play. Joy expands thoughts and actions. Joy facilitates learning new thoughts. Joy provides new cognitive and behavior skills. Joy forges new social relationships. Joy attunes to possibilities for relating to circumstances. Joy sees them in new light. Joy gives a sense of blessedness with progress toward goals. Joy is an enduring fruit of the Spirit. Joy is not disturbed by external circumstances. New Testament joy is of a different kind. Joy is an exceptional human experience. Not connecting joy as a robust phenomenon means no insight. Joy cannot be created.

This book calls us to a quest. God's gift of joy brings purpose, power, production, and peace that is beyond understanding. How do we lift people? "Walking each other home" ignites joy in the heart of God. This writing discusses what it means to lift each other. Joy comes at the finishing of the journey. We are all created to be sisters and brothers. Nobody walks alone. To ordinary people, joy is known only in patches. These sheds have been assembled in different patterns. Self, others, and scholarship in theology, psychology, and sociology.

It is not confined to people in famous universities. When a joy experience is gone, we compare that joy with present circumstances. Somewhere within people know they were created for joy. God is joy. God makes us into our true selves. Gradually and gently, Joy works within as God the presence discovers the divine in us. Humans spent time fabricating a false self. Allowing the Creator to remake us, we will be the best self we can be. God is within the world. This is the mystery of joy. Awareness of mystery is awareness of God. Discovering God in ourselves and in all creation mans sensing the presence of mystery everywhere. Mystery evokes wonder. Mystery is not a not a problem to be unsolved. Inadequate images of joy abound. Reverence is not made to feelings of joy. Joy is life, eternal life.

The joy of being exceeds the contentment with having. Joy includes feelings. Superficial expressions are not deep joy. The gradual and unrecognized growth of joy within is important. Emotional spasms and thrills are of little significance when joy grows within us. We perceive joy all around us. Joy within enables seeing through the disguise to the reality. Joy lies waiting with infinite patience for its appointed time.

Joy stays in a deep sleep needing awakening. Redemption is becoming awake to the joy.

Knowing God's joy within us recognizes joy around us. Our joy meets God's joy in the world. Joy comes as our artificially fabricated ego breaks down.

The quintessence of joy is an active exhilarating communion with God.

My prayer is that you find this book a blessing. It will reveal your own path to joy. My calling is to eliminate unhappiness. Walking in joy helps control moods. Soaring through the clouds joyous people discover the sunshine of God.

Bringing joy to God spins my soul. When I baptized my children and grandchildren, I pray over them as special. Parents raise them in the image of God. At the other end of life's journey, Jude tells us we will stand before God and see God's joy. Read Jude 24. God majors on impossible things. God is omnipotent. God never lies. Read Ephesians 3:20. God can do more than we can imagine. The Book of Jude places confidence in the unlimited power from God. Power to not stumble. Older people lack balance. Walking each other, eyes search for obstacles that cause a fall. God steadies us. God protects us from tripping. Read Psalm 94:18. Weak ancles causes stumble. Look deep within. The concept of presenting a soul to God "without fault" stirs inside. Read I Peter 2:24. Bringing joy to the heart of God is beyond imagination. God scrubs our scarlet stains. We become white as snow.

Jesus makes us pure. Standing before God, we will encounter the joy of God. God's heart will leap for joy.

Flourishing After the Pandemic

My family has been vaccinated. After this disastrous year of isolation, grief, and trauma, we wonder about creating an environment for joy. Walking with each other, we join those who are strolling from languishing to flourishing.

The end of the pandemic can be a restart for living. We can walk out of struggling lock downs to create a new normal.

As society raced from flip phones to new smart phones, few leaders were concerned about the difference in living. The pre-pandemic revolution increased the influence of consumer culture. Big tech influences young people and older ones.

Churches are shrinking. Attendance and giving are declining. Declining levels of participation can't be blamed on the pandemic. Big tech shapes how we live and move. Flourishing is now perceived as a consumptive way of life. Be aware of notions of what the Good Life means. We need to recognize our immersions. Seeking a new way, we thrive if we know "the joy of the Lord is our strength."

Celebrate with others as we prepare to go home to heaven. I gave the invocation and benediction on Memorial Day to honor veterans and a rebirth of freedom to live with others not alone by ourselves with no guidance. We are wired for connection. Create a new normal. Find a sense of what is important. Stay committed to enabling neighbors locally and globally to flourish.

Comparing ourselves to others and getting stuck in the maddening mud stuck in jealousy or competition will bring no joy. With the gift of joy, we create space to do the work we love and are guided toward doing.

Too many people live lives that are meaningless, weak, contentious, powerless, and angry. God created us to have stamina for every circumstance, well-being during duress. We are to live above conflict and strife.

The Spirit of God is upon us. So be it.

As individuals and in community, we keep joy throughout every season. This book aims toward spiritual transformation. We learn, accept, experience, share, interview, research, converse, and pray. My intention is to transform individuals, congregations, and the world with a clear vision of joy from the periphery to the center. My words are stimulation of what God would communicate to you.

Everyone is born. Everyone dies. We vary in conceptualizing death. Death is a transition to another form of existence. As we walk with each other, we influence the fear of death, willingness to die for a cause, expressions of mourning, and the means of a celebration funeral.

Discussion about birth is accepted. Death is a highly reluctant topic. Defining death is not easy. Most accept the medical definitions. What exactly happens when we are dead? We shed the body. In faith, we co-exist with the departed. Loved ones influence the well-being of the living. Death is not an abrupt permanent disengagement. Death brings significant implications of how we act in living.

Death Anxiety: Fear of Death

Walking each other home involves fear of death. Humans refuse to contemplate reaching the end of earthly sojourns. The common is response is fear. Self-preservation drives us. Becoming self-aware, future outcomes are anticipated. Death occurs at any time. Anxiety and utter terror reminds us of the inevitable. Humans do everything possible to continue living.

Talking and listening about visions of heaven, some are simple. Some glorious. Seeing gates of the glory of God open wide and streets of gold are depicted. Others talk of eternity with friends and loved ones. Seeking definitions of heaven, some see uninterrupted divine contemplation. Ten or a million times more than anything on the earth. Few even try to grasp the grandeur and beauty. The joy of heaven is beyond imagination. Visions of heaven are dreams fulfilled. The joyous journey to that land that is foreign and familiar might feel like we have been there before. It might be like in the Wizard of Oz when Dorothy clicks her heals and says, "There is no place like home."

Like joy, heaven will be a surprise. The profoundest loss is the treasure we despaired of ever finding. The realization comes that we know that we were there before our birth and the time after death.

Heaven, our eternal destiny, is worth deep meditation. Imagine. Remember a moment of captivation of beauty. Envision wind blowing through lovely trees. Heaven is pure beauty. Better than all beautiful moments combined. These continue endlessly. Remember a time when you had great health. Pain free. Rested, energetic, and enthusiastic joy.

Heaven is perfect health forever. Think of an occasion when time stood still. Remember being caught up in a piece of music. Crashing of waves mesmerized your walk on a seashore. A fascinating play or movie riveted joy. Heaven is pure love.

Remember an intimate moment of prayer. Feeling close to God in a mystical union, we feel connected to God forever.

Joy exceeds imagination. Eternity never ends. Pondering heaven, we grasp the meaning of eternity.

Imagination is eyeing something greater than ourselves. Heaven is eternity of being our true selves. We are loved. We are committed to God's purpose. Infinite love brings on love as we never have felt. There is no burn out in heaven. Heaven is communion. Exhilarating. The joy of communion means talking and being with all through the centuries.

Heavenly joy means opening up to all that love can experience. True self will be revealed. Respect of each true self is to reveal who we are. Most are inclined to self-censor dreams of heaven. That's normal. One day we will meet each other in heaven.

Staying alive contributes to the continuity and socialization of the species. Death anxiety becomes a destructive force resulting in spiritual, mental, and physical problems. Walking each other home, we conceptualize the fear of death of oneself and the death of others.

Avoidance is one way. We try to do activities that defy death. Skydiving, rock climbing or going to war are examples.

A few people deal with death in funeral parlors and retirement homes. Physical appearances change with plastic surgery. By incorporating materialistic views, we equate death of body with death of self. Fearing a prolonged and painful dying process is a rational response for older people. Believing in an after-life, brings less anxiety. Those expecting punishment in hell display higher death anxiety than those expecting getting a heavenly reward. (James Gare, "How Death Initiates Life: Cultural Influences in Conceptions of Death, *Psychology and Culture*, pp. 6-32.)

My vision and quest are for exploring spiritual frontiers. My books are addressed to regular people. I have shared victories and defeats with other regular people. We shared in wakes, in joy moments and grief.

The Church and our country are at a pivotal point. The decisions we make will set the direction for generations. We enjoy inviting people to discuss important issues. We invite you now to come to our new home. We shall share a cup of coffee or tea, intimate prayer, and discussion around our kitchen table. Living in joy is the kind of life we read about in the scriptures. It is possible. We have been dangerously with a casual faith. Our experience with the joy of the Lord will lead us to be living illustrations of justice, love, and compassion. We are formed in the image of Christ for living as he did. Spurgeon preached "Wherever the Spirit of God comes, there will be joy in the church and life in ministry, in family, in prayer, and within an indescribable peace."

I have come to realize that I have been used as an instrument of God I have received more invitations to share. Hundreds of letters of appreciation have flown in from throughout the world. My books have been translated into many languages.

Joy is a pleasant state of quiescence. We feel joy when we achieve a goal. Graduating from high school or college brings joy. A joy came to me when my daughter Linda was named valedictorian at Central High School in Saint Joseph, Missouri. Besides my own graduations, I had joy when my grandson graduated from a Maryland magnet high school.

If you feel suspicion about being encouraged to enjoy life more, I promise I'll never write something that deceives you. The idea of living joyfully seems too good to be true. After his resurrection, Jesus said to Mary, "Mary, do not hold on to me. I am ascending to my Father, to my God and your God." That's what heaven is like.

Eternal contentment may be our goal. We do not have to wait until heaven to enjoy your precious life. Augustine said, "Love God, and do as you please." He meant that if we love God, we will strive to do what pleases God. We can never afford to be self-centered. In following in God's directions, we discover fullness.

Joy is central in the understanding of the Good News. In this book, I have shared my appreciation of Julian of Norwich. I used her words to inspire my love and joy. "The greatest honor we can give Almighty God, greater than all our sacrifices, is to live joyfully because of the knowledge of the love of God."

People have criticized me and preachers such as Norman V. Peale, Billy Graham, and many of secular and religious fame, because we say joy is more than a feeling of wellness. Joy comes from inner knowledge that God is living in you. We are carriers of love. The Spirit will cause us to share it.

Pleasures may be here now. They will be gone and forgotten tomorrow. The knowledge of God's love is not a feeling. In a Recovery session, using the methods of Abraham Low, we might hear, "Feelings are not facts" many times. Low is the founder of Recovery International. It helps emotionally disturbed regain mental health. Feelings can be upsetting. Feelings are not truthful.

The least of the brethren feel. Slavery was soothed with joyful singing. Their joy put the masters to shame.

The early Christian martyrs sang joyfully just before they were led to their deaths. Their joy was possible because it was given from God above. By the grace of God, we learn to control fears and anger, anxiety and guilt. We live with joy because of love.

Joy enters the soul trough intimate prayer, bold faith and the will to bear discomfort, sickness, and death.

Some people never find themselves until the season of middle age or later. By relying on your instincts alone, you are certain to fail to know joy. When we listen to the words of Jesus and act on them, we shall find the place for receiving joy that the world does not have to give.

To experience joy in the middle of your soul to the surface of your smile, you need, as Abraham Low would say, "to exercise your joyful muscles." Drink the joy. Live the joy. Go and be a minister of joy to the world.

Come go on a vision quest with me.

Joy is the sweet sign of harmony with the will of God. Sharing my quests for joy is setting souls on fire. Like fire, I gain energy from everything I experience. The fuel is consumed. Like fire I generate heat. Like fire, I spread in all directions. Like fire I dance in the air. Like fire I find heaven is now. Like fire, I hunger for more life. Like fire, I am obsessed for eternal life. Like fire, I am deeply consumed by joy. Like fire, I am filled with creative passion. Like fire, I consume everything good or bad. Like fire, I leave nothing behind me. Like fire, I inspire people with my intensity. Like fire, I warm people with passionate joy.

Writing this book gave a new dimension and understanding. Each section of this book shares the seasons of life. Joy is a gift from God. Desiring good for each other, seeing God in everything, seeking opportunities to bring God into our journeys is where joy exists.

Be grateful for free will that is lived with responsibility. Walk with people and in places where you can ask for help. Do something to change circumstances. Ask God and others for guidance. Change what you are saying to yourself about the situation of joylessness. Everyone is born with capacity for joy. Finding that seed of joy already inside you, start to nurture it. Nurturing at times reveals that a dream deferred is not cause for a defeating attitude. In murky haze, the future exists around the corner from the vision. Imaginings live on their own supplanting God fueling dreams. Reframing our perspective enables us to see clearly.

Dreams can be a gift from God. Visions might grow from the soil of untrustworthy hearts. A place to start would be to know our motives. If our dream comes true, who gets the ultimate glory? Dreams must fit the gospel. Finest dreams fall apart. Dreams deferred often explode. God may say "no," but the Divine will reframe it. Dreams become idols. Shift the focus to the will of God. In that spirit, we discern the unexpected ways dreams were fulfilled. God's ways are not our ways. The thoughts of God are not the same as our thoughts.

When designing my new home, I had a beautiful stain glass with a frame built into the wall between my office and the bedroom. The frame transformed the stain glass art. Reframe what others say. Think about the real message they are sending. Search behind their words.

One of my joy times was experienced while writing in a journal a letter to God. Words began to flow. I wrote for hours. When I finished, I realized that God cared for me. The process of writing has its own rewards. Earning a professional degree from the University of Columbia School of Journalism before seminary was therapeutic, educational, and self-empowering. Writing is a technique to access subconscious imagery. Psychotherapy is as individual as a particular therapist.

Keeping a journal enhances progress in a counseling session or in between sessions. A diary is the only form of writing that encourages total freedom of expression. Encouragement of honesty leads to more discoveries triggering joy. Journaling is an ideal context for continuous confrontation. Writing accesses an inner source that is usually hidden from human conscious. Realizing where we are in a particular season, we tap into the next season.

My professors at the University of Missouri taught that writing helps solve problems, survive difficult seasons, and create a healthy expanding life. The best journalism students used logic, intuition, and creativity. Writers write despite challenges inherent in the writing process. They go through multiple drafts. They seek the opinions of other writers. Unavoidable, less interesting mechanical parts of writing include paying attention to grammatical details and proof reading.

I enjoy writing. I am drawn to that particular joy. That phrase in the movie, "Chariots of Fire" reflects just how I think as I write: "God made me fast and when I run, I feel God's pleasure."

When I write, I am totally absorbed. I am oblivious to any distraction. Time passes quickly even if I write for twelve hours straight. During life, I have written millions of words.

Joy comes in the published product. The real satisfaction is the writing. When my main ministry was writing at the Sunday School Board, I recall writers describe writing as self-transcendence, self-absorption, and qualities of joy. These include spiritual and intrinsic value, absorption, rich perception, disorientation in time and space, and lack of the usual fears and anxieties. These joy moments are perceived as pure and innocent, almost child-like. Confidence in communication, as the flow of words without the sense of time. After I finished *Joy Comes in the Mourning*, which is about my younger brother's death, I started crying for twenty minutes. Crying brought catharsis.

Writing gives me insight about life and how writing such as the Bible gives me knowledge and direction. The need to uncover or discover a mystery is deeply rooted human characteristic. Writers experiencing joy differ from writers who lack that experience.

My brother David wrote an extensive book of the McReynolds family. It is a legacy for every member of my family. What a joy to know that something as personal as written evidence of thoughts makes sense.

Loved ones communicate with you.

David came in the energy and form of a butterfly as I described in *Joy Comes in the Mourning*. Other signs include a vision of my once wife Nancy walking towards me in the hall of my home.

Dreams are the most frequent path for loved ones to connect. Dreams from the heavenly home are incredibly vivid. Communication is received in dreams to say they are happy. They appear vibrant, regardless of their state when they died. The dream ends. Loved ones live on. Pay attention. I feel my loved ones looking out for me. Sensing them in the air, feeling watched, or somehow letting us know they are with you. Smelling a familiar scent such as their favorite perfume, food, or drink, lets us know that we are not alone.

During my years of research and ministry, I have copied down how people I encountered described joy. Some were awesome such as merging of action and awareness, immediate feedback, unconcerned about failure, lack of distraction, balance between challenges and skills, and absence of self-awareness. Piecing together all these perspectives was like putting together a 1000-piece jigsaw puzzle with family or friends. Our family has been putting together jigsaw puzzles for many life seasons, especially during the cold and storms of winter. One puzzle had four shades of orange, four of white, four of green, and four of maroon colors.

All God's children fit together. Each has individual qualities with a common purpose. Gifts we are given help calm nerves, comfort share reassurance. Focus on your particular piece. Zero in on it. It's your purpose in the body of Christ and in circles of friends.

On the path to passion for crafting kingdom joy, thank God.

Fanning the Flames

Woodlawn Baptist Church in Bristol embraced me unconditionally. My home church was an immense encouragement to me. They believed in me and told me so. On their 100th birthday as a congregation, they asked me to come share my ministry of joy. Spurred on by the members who took their time to notice my good qualities and to overlook the faults.

Most of the members when I was there have died. When I spoke at the centennial, I noticed a woman who taught me in Sunday School. Talking to her about future options, she laid out some pros and cons. She listened patiently to my thoughts. What continues to impress me is that she told me what she was thinking about. She assured me life would turn out well. Her words warmed my soul. She ended by saying, "Besides, I believe in you."

Fan the flames of love by letting people know they are included in your prayers. Tell them you believe in them. Use your home, your resources, and your warm-heartening words.

Fan the growth of souls. Provide a listening ear. If they are comfortable doing it, pray with them before they leave your home.

Lift up concerns and believing together with them for answers. When traveling in airplanes, I often have to buy a ticket that has at least one, if not two or three layovers. I spend hours during layovers. Sometimes layovers help me catch my next flight in airports such as Chicago or Atlanta. I can read a book. Time passes slowly on travel hiatuses. I find a coffee shop or café. I order something hot in winter, something cold in summer. I enjoy talking to the people. I meet fellow believers. Seeing smiles, I realize that what might be a humdrum day of travel turns into an adventure.

I enjoy reading New Testament letters. The writers open the letter with greetings. The recipients are honored in a unique way. Paul wrote in Philippians 1:3, "I thank God every time I remember you." Whisper a prayer as we are grateful for all the people who serve us. Gratitude keeps our eyes and ears alerted to those whose hard work goes unnoticed.

Do ministry with the mailbox for those far away. Revive the forgotten art of handwriting on paper. Send a handwritten note to a faraway friend of family member mentioning what you appreciate about them. What a joy to write a grandchild on a birthday, graduation, or for special honors or accomplishments. We are walking each other home.

C.S. Lewis walked in all life seasons with the thought, "You can't go back and change the beginning, but you can start where you are, and change the ending."

Walking is free. All of us can find a place to walk. Moods and emotions become lighter. Focus on the senses as you pass. See the world, on foot, in contact with surroundings.

God designed human beings to walk. Walking in the Garden is written in the Bible. Walking is natural. Bodies and minds protest when we no longer can walk. Obesity, diabetes, mental health disorders, and joylessness result from not walking. If we do not move, one day we won't move.

Walking calms and restores cognitive and emotional reserves. Walking with others yields togetherness. It is one way to know others. Stopping to wonder at an unusual flower, we increase our social connection building a bank full of shared experience.

Walking is flourishing. Churches can hold meetings or pray while walking. Helpful ideas come while walking. Being outdoors allows the mind to rest.

Plan to walk in every season. If you travel by bus or cab, get off the ride early. walk the rest of the way. Make use of lunch breaks. Go for a walk. Find a walking buddy.

A Prayer for Joy

Heavenly Father, how I bless and thank You for the glad tidings of great joy given to all people. Thank you for the angelic host that sang celestial joys. Thank You for Jesus, and the joy and peace that floods the souls of all who have believed in him, the rock of salvation.

Eternity is too short to praise and magnify Your glorious name is goodness and love and fullness of joy.

Help me to share this joy of knowing Jesus with all those who walk with me. I pray there may be sinners today who are saved by grace through faith in the shed blood of Christ Jesus, so that they too may experience the joy that is available to all who believe in the gospel of grace. Amen.

Introduction to Joy

During my time at Christ College at the University of Oxford, I was given a card in which was written, "From joy all beings came, in joy all beings live, to joy all beings came, in joy all beings live, to joy all beings return." These words inspired me as I completed my dissertation to credential my ministry as a licensed mental health practitioner. "Integration of Joy in Clinical Family Counseling" was the title.

Seasons of Purification

The music changes. Songs of praise are new. Seasons change. Love remains. God works toward purification. Seasons bring new beginnings. Walking with each other in regular fellowship, we sense God within. Isolation stifles. Journeying with other children of God brings relief. We know we are not alone. Working with God in each season reveals the difference of each season. A tree does not bare all its fruit in one season.

Seasons take time to merge. Weather cools. Weather warms up again. Weather cools again. Some seasons are like a bow and arrow. Stretching back further and still further, the arrow fires an accurate shot.

Seasonal storms strike. Families stay locked down. Life moves in seasons. Season changes bring less activity during the pruning for purification.

Finding the joy of eternal union with God included perfect beauty. Our journeys are dress rehearsals for the next life. During my lifetime, international travel has brought unexpected warmth and connection. Somehow with the help of our family military officers, I have been blessed to share the joy of the Lord throughout the world. Travel allows us to reflect on our relationship with God, and to share God's promising words. Much like Rick Steve's says, "Keep on traveling for the joy of it." International churches increase desire to experience a joyful congregation.

Acceptance, Love, and Joy

When people think of love, they think of romantic or familial love as a feeling. Love is more pervasive and mysterious than a feeling. I once encountered a seducing woman who said, "Love is a feeling. Sex is a sport." She also said, "Nobody can love you like I can."

Love was obscured for her. It was out of her reach. Accepting love as a lifelong commitment that moves from fear, hopelessness, anger, and hate to strength, courage, trust, peace, and joy. Accepting "the joy of the Lord" takes you in a blissful boat from one shore to another. We stop efforts, and it comes to us when we do not expect it. Joy is a grace, but a grace in which we play a part. We create the atmosphere for joy to happen.

Accepting that God's love on our spiritual walk is vital. Our lives hold a host of unknowns. New challenges and opportunities come each day. God's love is a constant source of strength. What joy comes with the solid rock to stand on. Love overcomes all obstacles. Energy conquers all. See beyond the immediate. Events do not lead to a dramatic climax. Marching forward on our journey to joy, we feel God working through us. As we help God accomplish what the divine desires, we draw closer. God's love is shed abroad in our hearts by the Holy Spirit. Romans 5:5.

When I walk with someone that I love, I talk with them. Fresh open air opens intimate conversation. Read Luke 24:19-24. Walking in the beauty of surroundings reminds of beauty in loved ones. Shoulder to shoulder we stroll. Walking with God in silence forces out life's clutter of complexion.

With childlike excitement I feel love as a clear perspective appears. Walking with my beloveds I come up with creative solutions. Walking with Jesus is talking with Jesus. Those two who were walking with Jesus in Luke's gospel were not aware that they were in the presence of love. Jesus knows each one well and continues to love.

I think of this when I hear the singing of "Have a Little Talk with Jesus."

Giving attention fully to anything other than thoughts about yourself produces contentment, peace, love, and joy. When we do that, we are no longer in a world of self to finding unity with life that gives us not the prison of the ego, but the palace of God.

Giving attention gives us power to enjoy the experience of life as we create it. This is an experience of not-doing rather than a doing. Stop doing what is normal or automatic to you. We feed our stinking thinking with more endless thoughts. We feel that stopping our doing brings about nothing, while the opposite is found.

Humans are thinking machines. Consider that all our thoughts are the same thoughts we had yesterday. We need pattern interruptions in place for making necessary changes. We make the same decisions. We do the same actions. The habit continues each day. New thought patterns create more positive directions.

Thinking or writing about three things you are grateful for every day will enhance your new ways of thinking.

We sink because of how we think.

Tens of thousands of negative thoughts cycle through the mind day after day. These small thoughts add up to much of negative thinking and self-talk. If our thoughts are positive, then we are more positive.

Thoughts have more power over our lives than we realize. If thoughts are anchored in pessimism, the attitude will sink in negativity. Through my struggles for faith, God helped me understand about the choice of dominion. It is within me. We don't have control over circumstances or others. I cannot change how life is.

Ships, huge barges, or sailboats do not sink because they are caught in a storm or because of towering waves tossing them about. They sink because water that gets inside their hulls. We have no control over the storms of life, the mistakes of our past, the way other people treat us, or the circumstances we endure. We can give control of our minds by how we choose to think. Storms of life do not get inside us and cause us to sink. God's joy is our strength to stay above the stormy waters instead of being tossed about or pulled under the current of negativity.

The reason many of us do not ask God for mind transformation is that we do not realize we are stuck in negative thinking patterns. We know we are stuck in a mind-set of negativity. We are chained to victim mentality.

We can ask for nothing more important than for God to renew and transform our minds. When we ask, we are promised to receive. Life brings on difficult storms and problems are inevitable. Our thoughts need not sink us. Caught in a whirlpool of emotions that appear to be dragging us further and further into darkness.

We sink because of how we think. We have an intimate pathway for having God help us strive for a transformed mind. We can come to think differently, feel differently, and live differently. Allow God to shape thoughts and joy can stay afloat even in the midst of the worst storms. A negative mind will never lead to a positive life. With divine help, we can reshape thought patterns and habits, and improve life by reclaiming control over thoughts.

As we think, so shall we be. Think about this.

Giving attention is becoming aware of our attachment to a thought or feeling even if it is not satisfying. This attachment yields a sense of needing to get involved especially if fear is involved. This attachment is real and tangible, a convincing mirage.

Creating an environment requires us to envision what we can do to not continue doing what is automatic. Notice when we are caught up in a thought, a train of thoughts, or an obsession or a feeling.

Stop feeding your illusions. During your pause, notice the attachment or desire to go back to that thought. Feel your attachment in your body. Feel the tightness, the darkness, the stickiness, the inner churning.

Miracles happen. Imagine yourself held and supported by God. The Creator gives people to support you, opportunities, information, things, guidance, intelligence, as well as your body signals.

Joy in life is eternal, not just fleeting. This earthly journey is immeasurably valuable. Treasure each moment for the opportunities for growth and service to others.

In my office, I have a bright yellow sign with the words, "Don't Postpone Joy." Joy is being the best self. Read Matthew 5:15-16. Smile when you become aware of being gloomy. God is working in you with eternal joy. We are called to seek first the kingdom. Pray as if everything depended on God. Act as if you are the one responsible. Enjoy your gifts now. Heaven has started in you. Unimaginable dark events such as bombing the New York towers and today's world pandemic injected a fire in us. We did not postpone joy even in the midst of death. Dark feelings of the moment did not deter our courage. Postponement is like buying a huge amount of fresh fruit, but never eating it. Soon it rots. We can hold on to gratitude in all circumstances. Read Luke 11:28. Fear postpones joy. Weather the storms of life without losing connection to that which gives joy.

Looking for the Perfect Ministry Job

Fear of not finding a position or job yields disappointing terror. Every day I encounter individuals who are paralyzed from moving forward because they obsessively look for that perfect job. The fear of missing out on finding the purpose and place where God, you, and others desire your gifts seeps into the journey.

Joy is loving and serving family. Joy is service to the larger family. God's love flows through being forged into a vessel.

Indecision leads to joylessness. More than a few jobs will be part of your trajectory. Some of the churches where I have served, I would have enjoyed for 50 years. Free will and our human choices includes more than one shot "to do the right thing." Finding a joy-giving job is finite. Nobody just becomes something and that's the end. God lets us decide what life we want to design with the Divine creator.

Pray and follow intuition as you discover the boss of an organization is a selfish jerk. Remember, you are interviewing the search committee, the team you will be working with, the publisher, and the atmosphere where you will be giving a chunk of your life.

Narrowing choices down brings an element of loss. Nobody can hold 30 different jobs at one time. My most rewarding jobs have come with a surprising phone call. God might have been aware of it, but I know I was not.

We do not live in a fantasy world. Reality therapy is needed to wake us up. Don't look for a feeling of joy. Begin by believing the Spirit living in you. Be an instrument for sharing joy.

Tragedy will not result in complaining and whining. Actions have more power than words. Remain faithful to the choice to be joyful.

One day we will leave our bodies here, we will continue living. We take with us knowledge, wisdom, and talents we enjoyed on earth to the next place. Our soul embraces our challenges and desires. We have the resources to benefit from every experience, regardless how painful. We are transformed by every experience.

Heaven differs from the earthly existence. The Bible is filled with descriptions of the joy. Read the following verses to ignite hope during these pandemic times: Matthew 7:21-23, 25-46; Luke 12:33, 15:7, 23:43; John 14:3; I Corinthians 2:9; Philippians 3:20-21; Hebrews 11:6, 13:14; Revelation 7:9, 21:4, 9-12, 18-19, 22:1-5; Psalm 33:6; Isaiah 35:5, 65:21.

If only we knew the excitement, the enthusiasm, and joy our souls feel for this gift of being alive in the world at this moment. Step out of the human perception and we feel the joy, the awe, the wonder, and the love for this life.

This moment, whatever season we are in today, was designed for us as a way to know the joy that is in us. Feel God's pleasure in this. The journey passes quickly. With an eternal view, life passes in a blink of an eye.

Joy comes from God. While most emotions come from external sources, joy comes from within. It is always inside us. Our baby children delight in the simplest things. They never feign joy.

Becoming like a child rejuvenates the spirit. It brings fresh wholeness. Joy allows us more lightheartedness, more laughter, and more uninhibited playing.

As a child I listened as joyful children sang, "I've got the joy, joy, joy down in my heart. In repetitive fashion the song explains how joy exists down in our hearts. Thinking about joy is all the seasons later, the song comes back into my mind There is truth in these simple camp song lyrics.

Thinking joyfully, some hear confusion. Happiness depends on circumstances or happenings. It is not joy. We tend to attach joy to possessions or objects.

The human brain tends to focus on the negative. Take time to intentionally focus on ways to produce positive experiences to diffuse that negativity bias.

Acts of service are acts of love. These unselfish doings remind us that life is bigger than self. There is more going on than what we see and experience. Sharing this kind of love builds a sense of more intimate connection and belonging. Joy is a side effect of what happens when we act in the service of something greater than ourselves.

Accept the direction of unconditional love. Fear is the wrong turn. Fear keeps us believing what our thoughts tell us. What we think will cause us to sink. Thoughts have never helped us find our way, but they cause us to lose our way.

Over-involvement with the mind leaves us feeling hopeless and powerless. Life goes as it goes. We must learn to accept whatever comes. We cannot take life experiences personally. To enter into "the joy of the Lord," we give up our fears about what may be. The key to overcome these thoughts is staying in the present moment. Fear involves thoughts about the future.

Under the most difficult circumstances, if we live in the here and now, rather in thinking about a frightening future. Whenever we get caught up in thoughts, they lose access to the benefits of inner joy.

Fear activates the fight-or-fight response. This deactivates the part of the brain that enables us to reason and to tap into our intuition. Fear is an immobilizing state.

When we stay in the here and now, we gain access to wisdom and right action. We realize that we are eternal. We are deeply cared for, and the joy is like waking up from a nightmare into a beautiful world. Fear is an illusion. It serves no purpose. Accepting the strength of joy, we find that we never needed thoughts about the future. The future takes care of itself.

Because we rarely stay in the present moment for a length of time, this description of the present moment is perceived as unattainable and unrealistic. The monsters of our thoughts are illusions. Walk past them and enter the palace of the present moment. Our misguided perceptions keep us from being wise enough what is best for us are skewed by fear. Every fear has evolved into a desire.

We are blind to the desire to hold power over others. We fear poverty, so we do anything for wealth, not realizing hat wealth comes from love and the joy of relationships. We fear obscurity, so we push for recognition. We do know realize that all the recognition in the world will not make it erase the lack it feels. We desire to live on in monuments, not realizing that it never did exist. What is real is eternal. We resist the winter season of old age. We fear imprisonment, so we try to imprison those perceived as enemies. The real enemy is within.

The path from a self-centered life to becoming self-giving can be a slow process. Knowing our calling as a unique gift brings satisfaction. As we trust God, ordinary experiences are mystical. With no extraordinary qualifications, we know God will provide. Mystical experience is direct communication from the Spirit. God leads us in spite of our imperfections and unworthiness.

When we are sick, we follow the physician's orders. We rest in bed. We drink lots of water. We do not forget our pills. Shed those negative thoughts. Focus on accepting what can't be changed. Act on the things you can change. In joyful moments, God is present.

Unavoidable pain must be endured. Grace will help you accept with courage. Read Romans 8:35.

The grand purpose of our journey is to go home to God by reclaiming our inner divinity as a child of God. We came to earth for a reason. The reason is unknown for the life journey discovers purpose.

Light as many candles to feel light that lights thousands of others. Spread the joy. Create new ways to be joyful and to give joy. Play, sing, admire nature, dance, skip and tell others they are wonderful. In French, people express this *joie de vivre*, the joy of living.

Pray with me the prayer by John Killinger. "Lord, I am heartily sorry for the lack of joy in my life. I am too frequently tired, depressed, and annoyed. My life should be a continual paean of praise, for I have both heard and seen the coming of your eternal kingdom. Forgive my tediousness. Restore to me the passion of your salvation. Let me bear joyful witness to others of your transforming power. Through Jesus, who took his place among the poor and rejected of the world. Amen." (John Killinger, The Gospel of Contagious Joy, pp. 22-23)

Joy Is An Inside Job. Lovely women can keep smiling through an entire beauty pageant. Lisa Lester holds the world record of the longest smile at 10 hours and five minutes. Joy goes beyond a smile.

Cosmetics and smiling are found in happiness. Joy is deepest character. Joy is a human thermometer. Happiness is a thermostat. It registers conditions.

Joy is vital to faith witnessing. Nothing is a source of a powerful witness than the joy of the Lord. Cold dry faith has no appeal. Warm, winsome, and wining words attract people to joyous faith. Joy is important for walking with God. Joy lubricates life. Joy floods the soul. Joy energizes the body.

Knowing that there is no sin between you and God births joy. The burden of sin has gone. Intimate communion with God puts joy inside. This joy is not an imitation. Joy gives confidence. Joy lasts in losses. To rejoice is a choice.

Be fully present with important other souls. Make time for yourself. Establish a doable rhythm to be there with loved ones. Smile with kind eyes. Glance supportively to one being yelled at. Write a note to a child revealing how proud you are of them. A million little ways help you to be Christ's minister. Recharge your battery. Be generous. Connect with the flow.

Spirit of Joy Churches

Nothing keeps a joyful gathering from worshiping with enthusiasm. Connecting to them reflects their desire for you to know God. Smiles show honest, genuine joy. People share burdens and difficulties with God in prayer. Ministers and congregational leaders ooze joy. Dealing with disagreements they trust each other. Giving sacrificially results from trusting leaders and the vision.

Worshippers hang out before and after the worship time. They stick around and enjoy talking with each other. Unchurched friends receive joyful invitations to join them. It is not a place where members protect their home worship center from outsiders. A member who joined a year ago is as loved as a lifetime member.

They do not see the need for frequent business meetings. Each meeting is friendly and encouraging.

Walking with God and our fellow travelers brings insight joy.

Whatever view we take of life and death, we must know that the rewards of a future life do not prevent us from living life with zest and meaningful activity. Most believe that there is a life beyond death. Our lives may end in extinction. It is inconceivable to me as all I know is the consciousness of life.

Descending into the unconscious is frightening. It is like trying to cross a trackless moor in the night. We could fall on the edge into a disused goldmine. We could sink into a bog. Walls have to be broken down.

Churches of Joylessness

Spirit of Joylessness churches brings in the same devastation encountered in the workplace, marketplace, or home. The difference is that we do not expect people to behave like those without Christ. Joyless churches lack peace, safety, acceptance, forgiveness, and freedom from destructive conflict. Strife with hatred tarnishes the church established by God. Divisiveness gains control. Slowly and surely the infiltrated pain decays the church's foundation.

Joylessness begets misery. The church of Jesus goes about the serious joy of heaven. Joyless churches hold a perpetually low joy tank. Obedience is not in them. They are perpetually pessimistic. Counting it all joy keeps closeness at bay. Swinging verbal swords of sin, they cause joyful folks to put up the shield of faith.

The root of bitterness affects every fiber of the soul. God is not responsible for the behavior. Remember dedicated, loving, grace-filled people continue to be in joyless congregations. The most difficult church environment houses those hurt by church behavior. They and God hold inside themselves a compassion, a forgiveness, wisdom, and love. The focus shifts to God and off of other people and their disappointing actions. These resilient ones carefully guard thoughts, feelings, attitudes, and actions.

The bitter wounds fester and continue. Passion for God and churches dwindles.

We have to make another way. During this unconscious state, we will work in the darkness and shadows. Mystery surrounds our destination. It's like the dark that surrounds us. Our unease moves into nervousness. Life verges on panic.

My depression opened doors of my unconscious, allowing me to edit my life video tapes on which the unconscious has recorded the events of our lives. The tapes also reveal the feelings. Some feelings well up in our night dreams. Relief comes as we acknowledge them. Our maturing self can then take charge. I received integration of my personality. I learned to know my real self, not just the clamorous conscious ego.

Healing brings hope from the depth of the soul. That healing arises in love. The love looks horror in the face and goes on loving. Carl Jung calls this the shadow. My shadow side contains a mixture of feelings that I needed assistance to express. I was not responsible for those feelings, but only what I did with them. I was not to become falsely guilty for dealing with them. I allowed them to bring on a false guilt that built up a head of steam until they burst out in inappropriate ways at inconvenient times and caused my exhaustive breakdown. Negative emotions live in our shadow sides.

Gradually, I learned to name what I was feeling in the present and the past. I re-experienced feelings from the past, and they lost their hold on me. Repressed and unexpressed anger is the root for depression. Rage made me feel helpless. Healing comes from forgiveness, from going on forgiving the same hurts each time I become conscious of going on and forgiving seventy times seven and more.

Life reveals our purpose through certain people, experiences, and opportunities, and it closes the door on others. We make choices. We choose the specifics. We choose our attitude and responses. We cannot not choose the stage our lives continue.

Life is not scripted or predetermined. Life is steered, guided, circumscribed, shaped, and determined by particular events that are meant for you.

We are given free will for a reason. Life is not here to support personal will. Free will is part of the plan in which our individual will is a small part. The more the personal will is aligned with a higher will the more joy that is identical to "thy will be done on earth as in heaven."

The divine spark is our gift for not going in wrong directions. Our journey has been divinely designed by loving forces. What we believe, we will sense that God respects our free will, allowing us to make choices and to experience the results of those choices. If we are aware of nothing but the physical than we will never act beyond senses. The only desires that are meaningful are associated with reality.

"Thy will be done" is not experienced as "I want," but it comes as an urge, a drive, a peaceful feeling, or inspiration that moves us in a particular direction. Something that is alive in us comes from the divinity inside us that knows that it lacks nothing. This mysterious something is "they will be done."

God created the mind to explore, imagine, create, and direct us. We are beings that are curious, fascinated by life. As children of God, we can use our minds to replace the useless speculations, perceptions, and fantasies.

In a marriage, acceptance means that your love is so great and so deep that there is nothing the two of you can do that will disturb each other. Where acceptance exists, all is forgiven and forgotten in the service of love.

Refusing to accept what is brings denial and judgment. We pretend a problem does not exist. Couples become critical, harsh, and condemning. We then lose the joy, the passion, and intimacy we desire. Transformation starts with acceptance. Without it, we hide and think everything is all right.

If something your partner is doing grates against you conditioning, then you need to look at your conditioning, and not try to change your partner. A marital relationship never involves changing people. Your only task is to love them.

Love requires letting go of a desire for your partner to be richer, stronger, smarter, or attractive, younger, thinner, voluptuous, neater, organized, and exciting. Until you give up your desires for your helpmeet to be different, they will interfere with your ability to love your spouse.

Become conscious of the ways you are withholding love because you find him or her unworthy, or because you think you gain something by withholding love.

That person in front of you is the person life has given you to love. You made a commitment to this person out of all the people that you encountered. You can give that person love or try to find another person.

You view your spouse in a certain way, which is quite different than reality, because the mind distorts and leaves out much of reality. You are blind to reviewing what you loved about your spouse and the things that attracted you.

We blame others for our unhappiness. We create our own misery. Nobody else is responsible for causing your happiness. Blaming and judging has no place in relationships. I often tell my clients, "Nobody's to blame. Everybody is responsible."

Enriching joy times takes a special combination of people. Those persons will have to continue to nurture that gift of love. We all have separate interests that you enjoy apart from each other, and you allow each to hold those interests. Your partner's cup of tea may not be your cup of tea. It doesn't have to be. Differences are good and appreciated for the joy they bring. Imagine being a source for others to feel the level of joy as you greet them.

Joy is walking into a house and seeing the eyes of a child light up when she sees you. She runs toward you shouting your name. Excitement, enthusiasm, and unbridled joy fires up with bursting joy.

A joy-filled spirit never speaks words to complain or discuss flaws when that person is not there. Words are full of awesome power.

What joy I have been given as I read words from my daughter Linda and my grandson Ethan when they were children. They smiled. They laughed. Reading helps children grow and learn. Reading humorous books and buying funny books for children sparks laughter. Blessings or criticism come with looks, gestures, and words. Heavenly joy flows with relaxing in a bath of love. God's grace is poured on us now and forever.

Heaven is both present and future.

As we walk along the life path, we are already in touch with the essence of heaven. The world is radiantly alive with the presence of God. Walk with confidence in gardens of life-giving love.

Shimmering sunshine awaken our souls, gently reminding us of delight. Trees and skies, flowers and birds evoke praises. At the end of life's journey, we will reach our destination. God is preparing us for joy in every season. We reach heaven in God's perfect timing. Read I Corinthians 15:20-23.

Paul Tournier, the Swiss doctor, wrote "Christ compares man to a tree, one must receive the divine life into him so as to bring forth fruit. All of these undermine man's integration in nature." Paul Tournier, *The Seasons of Life*, p. 11.

When I preach on this insight, I have shared a parable written by unknown author that I have named "Four Seasons of a Tree."

"There was a man who had four sons. He wanted his sons to learn not to judge things too quickly. So, he sent them each on a quest, in turn, to go and look at a pear tree that was a great distance away. The first son went in winter, the second in spring, the third in summer, and the youngest son in the fall.

When they had all gone and come back, he called them together to describe what they had seen.

The first son said that the tree was ugly, bent, and twisted. The second son said, no, it was covered with green buds and full of promise. The third son disagreed. He said it was laden with blossoms that smelled so sweet and looked so beautiful. He noted it was the most graceful tree he had ever seen. The last son said the tree was ripe and drooping with fruit, full of life and fulfillment.

The man explained to his sons that they were all correct. Each had seen but only one season in the life of the tree. The father told them that you cannot judge a tree or a person, by only one season. The essence of who they are, and the pleasure, love, and joy from that life can only be measured at the end, when all the seasons are experienced.

If you give up when it's winter, you will miss the promise of your spring, the beauty of your summer, fulfillment of your fall. Do not allow the pain of one season be a barrier to enjoyment of life. Do not judge life by one difficult season. Persevere throughout the difficult patches and better times are sure to come sometime later."

This quick story sums up the idea that we all are in one season or another. Plan and prayerfully design your life's journey. This will help you recognize your potential and your limitations. During the seasons we are living single, married, having children, and the empty nest.

Some seasons will be difficult. Going off to college, moving to another place, starting a business, getting out of debt, or sickness and death.

Other seasons could include divorce, another marriage, fighting a legal battle, depression, military deployments, or losing a child. Recognize the season you are living in. Accepting where you are enables one to be aware of the limiting factors. As we face challenges and difficulties, we either overcome them or they overcome us. It is a choice.

Where we live, how we cope, what we choose, and a mile long list of circumstances are not always seen as a choice. Our response is always a choice.

With the joy of the Lord as strength, we are able to hold sorrow and joy in a delicate balance of serenity and peace. Joy brings a fragrance of a harmonious life. Walking with God teaches us how to respond joyfully to an invitation to walk, talk, or sit together in grace. Count it all joy.

We enjoy being around dreamers. We feed off their optimism. Our own vibration rises in the company of visionaries. They see miracles. We are the sum of the company we keep. Spend more time with your children. They hold the power of optimistic imagination.

Within us we have the strength to respond easily and happily to the most adventures each season reveals. When we are sitting still, we hear the song of life pouring joyfully into our consciousness. Listen now. It is always being sung. You will catch a vision as you let your soul move with the divine singing of the songs of life.

Heaven is filled with music. See Revelation 27. We will sing with the angels. God will give you a voice so you can join the harmonious sound.

One of my favorite writers of English literature is William Wordsworth. He wrote, "With an eye made quiet by the power of harmony and by the deep power of joy, we see into the life of things."

Joy establishes each human so securely in the videos and photos in our transformed minds, that people can cope with whatever life throws in their path. Joy is the fire that keeps our purpose warm and our minds and spirits aglow.

I encourage the reader to be reflective at the end of each chapter. Prayers for joy that were part of my worship for more than 10 years at the First Christian Church in Weeping Water, Nebraska will be shared after each section.

Prayer for an Abiding Joy

God in heaven, what a comfort to read of the prophets of old who despite the difficulties they were called upon to face, were able to rejoice in the Lord Jesus and trust his never-failing faithfulness.

I pray that like them, I may receive your abiding joy and discover, like them, that the joy of the Lord is our strength. This peace is an abiding peace that enables me to overcome all difficulties of life in the power of the Holy Spirit.

Fill my heart with everlasting joy so that I may rejoice in life's circumstances, in periods of plenty and during those seasons when I have so little, in times of hardship as well as those times of sufficiency.

Thank You that You are both Father and Lord. May my soul rejoice in good times, in bad days, and may joy and perfect peace find residence inside of me. In Jesus' name. Amen.

Practical Application

Write a note on "What is joy?

Write a list of words that you associate with joy.

Begin a list of three things you are grateful for as gratitude and joy are similar.

Take a walk for as long as you can. Be attentive to how good you feel.

Prayer the prayers at the end of each section.

Paint a word picture with Jesus as you walk with him.

SPRING

"The Christian thanks God whatever happens, in the sense that nothing can render God pointless."

--Soren Kierkegaard

Spring

Spring brings fresh feelings. Springtime is a new zest. The unstoppable feelings honor spiritual spring. Winter's new ideas and plans emerge. With those clear thoughts, we are ready to handle whatever may come.

During the first stage of life, from the day of birth to the twenties, there is growth and maturity. Spring nourishes. Education happens. Counselors give insight.

Colorful iris flowers flutter. The ruby red plum buds. Winter's blizzards blast smothering blossoms. Springs stirs slices of slumber. Colors like green paint the lawn. Spring showers smell sweet. Awakening from spiritual hibernation, we give the spirit a fresh try. Sun shows splendor. Spirits start soaring.

Spring marks the end of harsh winter. Spring brings a liveliness as flowers bloom. Trees have fresh green leaves. The sky is clear and blue. What joy to watch colorful butterflies hopping from one flower to another in the garden. The ponds, creeks, and rivers flow again as they are free from being frozen. Between eggnog and ice cream, we enjoy more in the light. Light is natural as we join in walking each other home. We sense the love for ourselves and others.

Loving God and Loving Ourselves

Music, poetry, magazine articles, and books echo the words, "All you need is love." Bombarded with ecological and natural disasters, wars, greed, and pandemics, we fail to fortify ourselves with love. I pray unconditional love will be enough to gift my children and grandchildren with joy. My calling and the purpose of this book is to spread the news that love is the most important force for good. Love begins inside and it is our responsibility. Love is uplifting and healing ourselves. Love expresses by this self-touching and healing. The body is in the soul. The soul is in the body. God is in the soul. The soul is in God. Jesus is God's invitation for being united. Christ is God's blessing. We have not been forgotten. False dies. True soul is born. Soul is deeper into silence. Soul is free. Soul knows God. God's presence is known.

As children, the world revolves around us. Negative thoughts like we are not important, good enough, worthy, or smart enough. Sensitive people are made aware of the way we dislike or even hate themselves. People who are supposed to care about us the most miscommunicate and mistreat during impressionable childhoods.

Opening ourselves with the joy of the Lord strength promotes intimate relationships, harmony, and well-being. Become aware of decisions based on unique experiences. We continue to write our life scripts. We might need professional help. Self-love appears overwhelming. Become aware of internal and external surroundings in order to find enlightenment for ourselves. Loving yourself as God loves builds the foundation for loving God and others. Joy is touched. Relax. Breathe.

Speak from the conscious true self. Say "I am a loveable person." Human beings tend to encrust themselves with layers of stubborn will. As layers accumulate, awareness of the divine core, true self, gradually diminishes until it is forgotten. Souls petrify until there is no strength to halt the ossification by ourselves. The central theme of the book of Romans is the inability to chisel a way out of the self-imprisonment to chisel a way out of the self-imprisonment in chunks of dead stone.

Glorifying God and Enjoying God Forever.

Honestly, have you ever read a better book for approaching the life-affirming, loving and transformative process? Rely on the wisdom of people who embody unconditional love. God's still small voice guides us to experience the depths and heights of the journey. Loving myself makes me at one with everything in my atmosphere.

My goal is to be fulfilled on earth now and eternally in the next place. With joy inside, I attract loving relationships. Love-filled souls fit my gifts, my talents, my feisty ways assisting me to drop negative thoughts. Being at home with myself, I hear a symphony of love that resonates a strong light ray of energy into the world. Let God love us.

Now true self is here. It is loved by God. It is freed to love. Reading God's book, I see with the eyes of God. I prefer the will of God.

Choose the will of God. Open the eyes. See the true self. Looking and seeing are one. When the eye is single, the whole body is in joy. Feel yourself alive. Love all willingly. Realize eternal life. Drop the false. Live the true. Life is not a torment. Life's journey is lived one day at a time.

Love is the meeting and interchange of spirit. Vulnerability and mutual self-disclosures begin at that crossroad. Love cherishes and honors faithfulness, fruit of the Spirit. We and God offer our intentions in uninhibited joy. Motives differ from intentions. Intentions reflect purpose and disclosure. Unconditional joy results in revealing the mystery and uniqueness of self.

The human spirit is the core of the self as desiring, longing, cherishing, believing.

The growth and development of self means our spirit selects by assimilating from all experiences. The inner spirit wills and resists, opens and closes, gives and receives. Trusting God's wisdom, we find insight into what is most precious in the human adventure.

Enjoying God focuses on all the good things in life. Enjoyers of God benefit from the grace of God's salvation. Enjoying God is the presence of the Holy Spirit. Enjoyers with answered prayers know God is always available. Enjoyers are determined to rejoice. Enjoyers relish salvation through Jesus. God takes joy in salvation of humans. Enjoyers luxuriate in the bath of good news. Enjoyers devour the biblical revelation. Enjoyers delight in the testimonies of God. Read Psalm 119:14.

God finds joy in us. Joy shows us full joy as God finds joy in us. Maximum exposure to the Word is walking with each other with God dwelling in us. Read Colossians 3:16. The Bible is joy-food for the joy-hungry soul. God sings over us. Read Zephaniah 3:17. We sing for joy in return.

Life is a mystery to be lived.

Life is not a problem to be solved, but a mystery to be lived. No matter how much we know and understand, there is more to understand. Mystery does not end with our own journey. Walking together we find others are a mystery. This world is a mystery. The ungraspable mystery enhances life. We listen. We learn. Wonder and surprise are part of the levels of depth.

John Killinger, who wrote the foreword to this book, shared part of his stories. He has been blessed in every season. As the readers reflect on his stories, create a story of your own.

Humans choose with care when, how, and to whom they share personal experiences. We are aware that life is sustained by Mystery. Our knowing falls short of the Holy Mystery who lives in all times and seasons.

Living mystery tells how unique each person is. Coming to live an adventure in this world, each has purpose and calling.

Each one has a relationship with the Mysterious Master who gives joy and love. Faith is the eye for us to see what we can only discern darkly. Self-discovery reveals our deeds, self-realization, and experiences. Read John 14:15. A biblical foundation for seeing into a soul is by deeds. Read James 2:5-17, 26. Motives and intentions for doing good works solicit joy. Or if not, they diminish the best deeds.

The world of a writer who reveals her inner world. The reader has a world of her own. Passing the time alone does not mean a growth in wisdom. The word "self" is too common.

There is self-enrichment, self-improvement, self-assertion, self-respect, self-affirmation, and self-help. We cannot love our neighbor as we love ourselves until we have a self to give.

Respect, love, and reverence for self as unique mystery and respect for others' mystery.

Life is a walk up a mountain.

Climbing a mountain is a gradual, ongoing process. Getting to the top is a joy moment. After that special moment is the valley of daily existence. Everything that happened before a moment of surprising joy is viewed as flowing from that experience. Returning to the mountain top is a memory stored. That mountain climb becomes a sign not only of past positive moments, but future moments. The search for God is not complete if it does not include others. The joy of life with Christ is not the pursuit of extraordinary experiences, but the loving service to each other. We share in God's vision of reality.

Sharing in the life of God causes us to become a new person. There is new comprehension of reality. There is perception of current reality. Noticing the divine presence, our knowledge is in human terms. The difference is not merely of degree but of the essence. God illuminates our judgments, desires, and expectations.

Every moment permeates with love and expectations of us. Everything that we experience is linked to God's love. By giving each talent, there is trust that we will take advantage of it.

God requests that we give everything in the sense of total self-entrusting. A gift returned to God comes back multiplied.

Life is a walk down a road.

Walking down a road is a metaphor for life. It indicates that we are moving with a goal and purpose at our own pace. Dignity and respect are given and received along the way. God is our companion in this walk. Read Psalm 18:36; 93:18. Picture other companions on the walk both living and deceased. Don't forget angels. Loved ones live within us. They abide with presence.

Physical absence does not end the indwelling. Loving relationships include those who died.

Unseen reality is revealed as we keep photos of those we love. When Loved ones are gone, they remain present and alive.

"Communion of the saints" unites all members of the family, past, present, and future. Reaching heaven means to be surprised. What a joyful surprise just to be there. What a surprise to know that we did not walk across the finish line by ourselves. And what a surprise to see face to face all those who helped us on the road.

Self-love breaks a feeling of self-importance. Sensing my personal power flowing through my veins, I am truly alive. My own abilities to work and play fill my passions. I deserve to be happy, healthy, and loved. By loving me, I accept life's changes and I stay energized and ageless. I enjoy humor. Taking myself lightly, I tune into the joy. Kindred spirits laugh and play with me. I have grown to be spontaneous, mindful, focused, and balance. Life for me is a gift from my loving God for my enjoyment. I breathe with knowing that "all is well and all shall be well," as Julian of Norwich says. I am love. I share love in healthy ways. My earthly journey has been a loving channel of healing love energy.

The human spirit inside is the integrating aspect of the soul, the real self. God offers us the vision and clarity to the mind and emotion. Life is breathed by God. Read Genesis 3:7. The breath of God is the spirit of God. In contrast the human spirit is an inverted loop of the divine Spirit. Read Proverbs 20:27. The fruit of love and joy is available. This joy discloses the spiritual perception that integrates the extraordinary into the ordinary. Joy brings the vision of purpose focusing on the whole of reality as deeper wisdom. Read Psalm 16:8-9.

The soul is the core of human spirit. The body is an extension of the self. Without the joy of the Lord, the self perceives abandonment and estrangement from the Spirit of God. Spiritual soul-healing is integration of mind, soul, and body into the core of life. Grasped by the power of love and grace, joy brings the assurance that nothing can destroy the real self. Read Romans 8:28, 38-39.

Knowing God is in control brings a peace, a calm, even in the midst of that which touches the core of spiritual being.

Drop all facades. Join together to create miracles. God is in love with each one of us as if we were the only one living on earth today.

Sleeping creature wake up. Shut things open. Seeds hiding in ground emerge. Sunshine works its magic. Awakening animals scamper in the woods. Babbling brooks dance again. Staying outside lets us see in the pathway, new fruits beginning to bloom. Green glades of variegated light reveal hidden freshwater.

Every creature that was asleep wakens. Everything shut opens. Every seed hiding in the ground emerges. Wakening animals scamper in the woods.

Spring cleaning rids our lives of detritus, things we do not need. Decluttering has benefits. This spring I unearthed storage boxes full of letters from readers of my books and sermons, books of photographs, post cards, notes, love letters. As I threw away baskets of clutter, I rethink my life in all its seasons through feelings of uncertainty and change. What is essential now? Spring is a season of hide-and-go-seek. Warmth comes, but then it's gone. Spring is fickle.

In Nebraska, we often have late March or early April snowstorms as we appreciate the exuberance of spring. By the middle of June, life busts unceasingly. We wake up each morning with a fresh sensation of wonder, awe, enthusiasm, and anticipation.

Suddenly the frost is behind us with warmer days, with beauty and color appearing everywhere. Roses, lilies, and more flowers than we can name, and they bring grace notes to miraculously transform the entire energy into breathtaking appreciation.

"Now let the heavens be joyful,
Let earth her song begin:
Let the round world keep triumph,
And all that is there:
Invisible and visible,
Their notes let things blend,
For Christ the Lord has risen
Our joy that hath no end."

--Saint John of Damascus

Having the freedom and means for travel brings joy. This joy brings us all the stimulation and sensual delights that travel provides. Every opportunity exposes us to majestic beauty that is life affirming, life sustaining, life transforming. Joy blooms when minds and hearts are fully alive with the charming beauty. Beautiful places are not just one moment of joy. Nothing we experience will ever be gone. Joy is the exotic perfume of another world.

Spring is a fickle season. Days move from loveliness to terror in an hour. Flood, wind, and a raging storm devastates.

During the spring, our family enjoys "love days." Often, we gift each other with symbolic, sentimental, or useful inexpensive things. It has been a family ritual in all seasons. We never get tired of the days a gift brings a "Why now?" To celebrate your being, to cause you to smile, add sentiment and pleasure to your day. That's why. Just to have a tangible object to touch, a fragrance to smell, or something to eat, or a bottle of wine are delightful experiences. A trifle of chocolate or a favored scented bar of soap brings joy. Spring echoes God's grace. Spring mirrors the profoundest images of heaven on earth.

Baylor's Joy During March Madness

Basketball reigns in early spring. As I had successfully predicted, Baylor University basketball players enjoyed the moment as the Bears won their first national championship in 2021.

Scott Drew had been honored as coach of the year with a 26-4 record in 2020 with a 23-game winning streak. Not only did he turn Baylor's hoop program into a powerhouse, but Drew created an atmosphere of joy to healing Baylor's athletic soul.

"We have been a Christ-centered program since I have been here," "said coach Drew. Everybody comes in, spiritually, at different levels. Each opens to growing. Each and every year, we want our players to grow academically, but also spiritually and in character."

Fifty years ago, I served as a graduate assistant in the religion department. It was pure joy to study there. I was especially blessed by John Davidson who taught psychology of religion. John was full of joy and faith. In the last few years, Baylor used its resources to establish George W. Truett Theological Seminary in Waco. ("Culture of Joy, *Baylor Magazine*, Spring 2021)

During the mid-week Baylor Religious Hour, students gathered to hear dynamic preaching from the best of the Southern Baptist Convention as well as ecumenical giants. Baylor's university choir brings a spiritual climate. They travel the world to share majestic music.

"Spiritually, whenever you go on a mission trip where you combine that mission with coaching, it doesn't get any better than that for me," coach says.

Joyful faith in the lives of student athletes in evident. All-America guard Jared Butler teaches a children's Sunday School class. Team captain Mark Wyble leads worship for home games. Coaches lead in prayer meetings for road games. In 2014, seven members of the team were baptized.

"Seeing the joy and excitement our guys play with is something that comes through the television for people out there. They see guys having fun playing, winning, playing well," Drew says with a smile. For Drew and his team, maintain the culture of joy remains a constant priority.

The coaches and players hold a clinic for the children from military families stationed at Fort Hood, a United States Army Base in Killeen, Texas. They share their joy throughout the community with a culture of joy. It's pure joy. It's fun.

The images of ear-to-ear grins and the hugs were not a stage act or gimmick, their love and joy are real. Drew says, "When watching the

Bears play, you can tell there is genuine love for one another. You can't fake that. The joy they share is definitely the key to our success."

I made my first international preaching trip to Juarez, Mexico with the Baylor Evangelistic Association. Baylor was like heaven on earth to me. The deeply embedded missions of Baylor carried to every corner of every program including athletics.

Living out the distinctly Christian commitment of Baylor's campus community runs parallel to Drew's personal journey.

Baylor's turnaround surprised everybody in the college basketball world. Scott Drew created an atmosphere for joy.

Joy wins. A physician friend is a devoted fan of Baylor University's basketball national champions. I sent him an email expressing congratulations. He had been so busy with Covid-19 issues that he had not watched the final game against Gonzaga. When he finally got to watch a re-run of the game, he was calm, not twisting in his seat when the score was close even toward the end. He knew who won. Joy won.

We cannot anticipate what the next life season will be like. Despite our journey's ups and downs, we are grounded in the joy of the Lord. We know who wins.

Jesus said, "Now is your time of grief, but I will see you again and you will rejoice, and no one will take away your joy." John 16:22. Joy wins.

Our distractions may have delayed our eternal blessing, but eventually joy wins with shouts of gratitude. Death brings grief, only to be swallowed with an everlasting atmosphere where joy never ceases to win. The joy journey is not without pain and disappointment, but the intensity of the down times increases the joy after the pain passes.

Once joy lodges in the soul, nobody can steal it away. Those stuck in a joyless cycle may not receive that glow of joy from our faces. God gives believers an infinite supply of joy.

Joy comes from the eternal insight of our inner self. Practice faithfully our love relationship with God and you will realize unlimited joy that we can never knew existed. Humans can become supernatural in joy as we practice our giftedness. Joy wins when our lives use the game plan of God.

When Ethan went to church at about age six, he asked his grandpa, "How big do you think the computer was that helped God make people?" It was another teaching moment for me.

I read Genesis 2:7. It's about God forming man from the soil of the ground and breathing in the breath of life. We are exactly who we are. We were designed that way in the image of God. Just like a young child, it is difficult to get my mind around the enormity of that creation. Each person is a masterpiece. When you feel unloved or unseen, ponder the truth. God individually crafted each of us. How inspiring and humbling it is that God chose to give human beings such elevated and important positions in the world. Read Psalm 8 and Isaiah 64:8.

When my brother David died, it did not feel like joy could ever win. The pain of his loss will never go away as I shared in my book, *Joy Comes in the Mourning*. Now, after a few years have passed, the joy of heavenly insight restored my joy, because joy is our strength. Joy will return. Joy wins.

Joy comes in the mourning.

During a support group, several pastors talked about their experiences of being forced from their pastorates. It is common to every profession to have to face rejection.

The group cited scripture such as Genesis 50:20 and Romans 8:28. A lifetime of experience is needed to face the hostility, the jealousy, the uncertainty, and gnawing questions. Church leaders' stories of shame and disappointment have become epidemic. It happens to good people. They only desire to serve God. Nearly 2,000 Protestant pastors and ministers are forced out of their appointments and callings every month in the United States. They are told to move out of the parsonage in two weeks. They receive not one dime of federal or state assistance, no unemployment money for them. Feelings of betrayal and guilt mix with feelings of anger, frustration, and helplessness.

God cannot bless a church that succumbs to cultural levels of incivility. Many of these men and women that have been hurt so deeply never recover. Some have spent the summers of their lives, paying out more than a hundred thousand dollars for seminary training to prepare for doing the calling from God.

During my ministerial years, I have encountered fully trained, ordained, and talented ministers who are uncertain whether to stay or leave the Church. Even ordinary members state the same with ambivalent feelings about the Church as an institution. Most of us experience the Church through the structures and practices of a particular church.

We stand at the edge because we are both attracted and repelled by Church. We are attracted to its founder and what he taught. We are repelled by many of the doctrines of the Church. Why do we see so many thousands of denominations? We can't help but to be attracted by Jesus' love. We are repelled by the power of the Church. We hate its dogmatism, its politics, and the self-righteousness. We are attracted by its invitation to on the pilgrim road. We are repelled by the fear-based insistence that it alone knows the way. We are attracted by some of its spirituality. We are repelled by the banality of much of its worship. We are repelled if and when church members pretend that they are better than non-members.

Lay church board members cause havoc for pastors. They act as if recent theological thinking must be kept from the people in the pews. If we offer new ideas or challenge established thinking or express doubts receive a hostile reception. Any challenge to the status quo evokes hostility. The traditionalists or ardent fundamentalists are slowly taking over and winning a larger slice of a shrinking cake. Church and politics of the culture lure people from energy that could be used to share the gospel.

Depression reduces the control over feelings. We now tend to avoid the services and sermons that upset or anger us. The case against the top-to-bottom, power-over models of authority talked about and evaluated. Church plants are defined by their differences from the main body. We live in tension between so many opposite views. Seasoned church people feel that they are tolerated, patronized, or even pitied. Our candles are unseen, the whisper of my joy is unheard. If my fire in my candle joins others with a warmer glow, the authorities turn away. If my quiet whisper becomes a shout, the church closes its ears.

Are our questions so threatening that they cannot be considered? Mainline churches have been both deaf and blind. Church allows only its art and its own music. It would be easier to give up our minds and give our wills to the current teachings and tradition. We all want to be accepted. However, we are not comfortable living a lie.

The comfort that church offers for full members may draw us in. We have to accept that comfort by compromising our integrity. We might find support from kindred spirits in our local congregation, but we must have to look further afield.

Networking with a minority has an advantage over church institutions. There is no formal structure or hierarchy. There is no education required, no theological ropes, no building, nor hate. It is a joyous comfort to find companions on our journey to develop friendship and soul happiness.

If we ask people to worship in a house church or church within a nursing home or prison, many will refuse. Those who journey into the proverbial wilderness become perceived as a threat to the church.

My humble suggestion is that we worry less about unity or uniformity of beliefs and give priority to the love of God which brings the joy of the Lord into the community.

Pretention creates pharisees. Joyless souls cannot love or be loved. They do not love themselves. They live in fear that their pretention will become exposed. Their shadow sides undermine relationships.

Whatever we need to confess our shadow characteristics that threaten and judge us with false images of God which lurk in our unconscious. There may be more to confess, but we can know that we are loved. God only loves. Growth pains are reality seeing. Physical health, rational concepts, and materialistic prosperity do not save us. Only love is joy. Live naked in now, this moment. Cling to nothing. Realize the true self. Living as the true self is the pearl of great price. Butterflies are not seen by caterpillars. Butterfly eyes alone see other butterflies. Every human is self-becoming. Knowing this we will see it in others. This is a single seeing. Eyes are windows. Eyes see beauty. This moment is eternal life.

Simply breathe in God's love. Let God form us. God is inside the self. The true self is inside of God. Jesus supports us. The Spirit renews the soul in his own image. Christ Jesus is God's self-image.

Walking close to Jesus is to become like him, to know what he knows as he knows.

True self is awakened in relationship. Realized in community, all the faculties of the soul are molded together. Love is rooted in love. Avoiding relationship is refusing God. Opening to relationship is life engagement. Attention is opened. Love keeps the will open and aware. Loving relationship is antidote for the misery of the false self. Humans are incarnated in a body, conditioned and formed in a body. Limitations cease at death. The will is freed.

The road to eternal joy is recognizing and doing honest living. Forgiveness is of essence. Practice loving relationship skills.

With joy, we are more at ease with ourselves. Love is now perceived with less duty and more joy. Joy becomes a way of reducing suffering. Joy enriches us to put our own suffering and disappointments into perspective, releasing energy for healing ourselves and those who encounter us.

The so-called Prince of Preachers, Charles H. Spurgeon, battled depression in all the seasons of his life. His preaching pointed to the difficulties of life and their potential for yielding joy. Good can come from evil. Many seasoned pastors become confident that they are better off now than if the pain has been allowed to stay at the church that forced them out.

Spurgeon preached, "Our afflictions are the highway that leads us closer to God. Our troubles are a fiery chariot to bring us to God, Afflictions, wave upon wave, will drive out souls nearer to heaven."(Charles H. Spurgeon, *Beside Still Waters*, p. 16.)

In the Hebrew language the term for joy means "bright" or "shining. "When walking with God, the deep, dark valleys can be followed by a period of brightness in which these precious souls keep on with joy as their strength.

Sustaining Joy in Tough Times

Trouble comes in batches. Life can be going along smoothly. Suddenly, life brings not just one obstacle. Several things happen at the same time. Why now?

Winter potholes caused four flat times in two weeks in winter in Lincoln, Nebraska. Two happened the same day. Flat tires can get fixed. The city can patch the broken holes. What an annoyance and expense. Flat tires became a crisis. For several weeks winter weather created trouble for drivers.

Charlie Brown in "Peanuts" cartoons said, "It always looks darkest just before it turns totally black. Life never goes as planned. We do not sail through without storms. Troubles come in the journey.

A chaplain in the army at Fort Hood, Texas had a sign on his office door. It read, "If you have troubles, come in and share them. If you have none, come in and tell me how you did it." Read I Peter 1:1-9.

Notice the phrase "you have to endure many trials." Persecution of Christians brought on miserable times. Emperor Nero burned Rome to the ground. Christians were blamed. Some were thrown to the lions. Troubles multiplied. Resembling Nazi Germany, Jews were ostracized. Homes were burned. Business places were vandalized with impunity. The air smelled tough times coming.

Taking our ego's point of view ends in suffering because our natural perception is incomplete. Suffering points us away from narrow perspectives. Life is telling you something. Our journey is like a school. Experiences are teachers. We can learn and grow. We do not always get our way. Life is not something to conquer. We desire control.

When bad things happen, they are personal. Difficult things happen. Wonderful things happen. Each is a part of the play. Fighting with life or fretting or blaming is useless. No matter what our thought stream spews out, you are in touch with deeper truths. We do not have to be bothered by thinking thoughts. We cause much of suffering without realizing it. Feelings take us out of the moment-to-moment flow. Inner wisdom is not available. Accept it. Stay present. We have what we need. Grace gives it from an external world.

Difficulties stretch us forcing us to develop inner resources. The best parts of us will be summoned. Suffering is kindness. Count it all joy. Souls choose extremely challenging experiences. Extreme suffering often wakes people from false perceptions. One answer to why bad things happen is that souls chose to have experiences. We are born into a world that evolves through suffering.

God knows, but we hold onto a false self with its false security. The ramshackle empire of our ego collapses. The deepest place of the true self knows nothing can separate us from the love of God. True self lives and breathes in abundance.

God's attractiveness is illuminated in the renewed self. God lures us as a Lover.

We feel like we are walking on water. Being still and silent in divine presence oozes into us the attractiveness of God. By discovering God's attractiveness, we find the true self. We are attracted by the real in the guise of the beautiful and the response is joy. True selves continue to flow from that joy. Life is just a continuing, spontaneous walk with God. The joy of waking each other home comes with risk. If one is to find joy, which is her true self, she needs to actualize what she is. Joy is her generous friend. When entertaining joy, she enables to find as her surprise something better and more satisfying than anything she could have imagined.

Why does life appear as unfair? People doing "bad" things are still blessed. Some appear to be rewarded for their behavior and greed. We think that our life classroom is filled with naughty children with no teacher to stop them. Lawlessness and greed prevail. Justice and sacrificial love are things we miss. Earthly journeys involve learning through trials and error.

We are given resources to solve problems. Other people are teachers. They can show you a way to joy. We tag life as unfair. That is how we awaken from illusions.

What can we do when fired from your job? Cancer, death, divorce, and other disasters! We are only passing through in the earth trip. This is not our home. When the heat is on, we look in an eternal view of life. Charles Trentham, senior pastor for the First Baptist Church in Knoxville, Tennessee received mail with the address as "resident. "Why that? He said I am not 'resident.' I am just passing through."

Life as we know it now will not last forever. During my years at Carson-Newman, I served with Dr. Trentham as student minister of prayer. I always envisioned having a church like his. Read Hebrews 11:16. We, as the scripture notes, are looking for a better place, a heavenly homeland. A few tears ago, I wrote to Trentham to thank him for letting me serve. He enjoyed my letters. He wrote, "Your letters are ones I'll take to heaven with me. Soon, I will go to my heavenly home." He died in a car wreck a few days later.

I feel the same about my cherished letters from my 50-year friendship with Dr. John Killinger. I have every letter and email he has sent.

In this world, things that are bought will wear out or rust through. Some of it will waste away or burn up. Some will be stolen or neglected. Clothing will become out of fashion, or simply cast aside. That is how it is in our perishable, temporary world.

God has given us an inheritance that will never perish, spoil, or fade. Heaven is incorruptible. Read I Peter again. Our inheritance will not be damaged. Our future home can "never perish." It will not be threatened by a tornado or violent storms. Nobody will break into it. We will not have to pay a mortgage.

Joy does not travel along the pathways that are known to us. Joy takes the road it fancies. Joy never takes the same road twice. Joy is free. When and if joy fails to rise like a spring of water, it is percolating another surprise.

In every season the redeemed in Christ will hold on to inexpressible joy in tough times. God reminds us that joy is not something that is reserved for heaven. Joy is in us at every moment, even now.

Circumstances may change. Callings in spring connect with sparks of joy, giving determination, scrappiness, and grit. Realizing that callings evolve as seasons of life change. Theologian and writer Howard Thurman expressed it best: "Do not ask what the world needs. Ask what makes us come alive. Go do that. The world needs people who have become alive."

Joyful magic comes at the intersection of the calling of God for being fully alive. Embrace who you are. Ignite the soul. Find God and yourself at the intersection.

Let God use your tough circumstances for divine purposes. Do not get sidetracked by temporary or petty things. In this life expect to face crummy situations. Whether the trouble is an overwhelming tragedy or just having a bad day, we can face them with joy.

Three universities that belong to the Pacific Twelve Conference have won more national championships than any others in the United States. Stanford has the most. Next comes the University of California at Los Angeles, or UCLA. Next is the University of Southern California, located across town from UCLA.

After being shellshocked 51-0 by Notre Dame, Coach John McKay of the Southern California Trojans said after the humiliating loss, "Men, let us keep this tough loss in perspective. There are a billion Chinese who don't even know this game was played." That's what comes with eternal perspective. (Steve Farrar, *Family Survival in the American Jungle*, p. 40)

When we find ourselves in tough circumstances, we continue to praise God. This kind of attitude will encourage others who are in tough situations.

In the spring of 1973, I felt rescued after being treated for exhaustion at Deaconess Hospital in Evansville, Indiana.

I was blessed by the nurses and physicians who led me out of a horrid period. Just as I found a path to healing from the description of Peter Brice's time of healing from dark depression in his book, I trust being vulnerable to sharing my own story will bring joy to those searching for it. Read Psalm 16:11.

Psychotherapy was done in a church community setting long before the young science of psychology was born. The goal was to tap into the miraculous, fulfilling, and ultimate joy. For the best and worst of us, life becomes a prison. That torture brings unfulfilled dreams, discouraging circumstances, and an unending dirge of emotions. We see only a black horizon. Finding my joy brought of new way of thinking, a fresh lifestyle. We look for joy in the wrong places. We think that impressive degrees, beautiful children, passports filled with stamps from exotic and faraway places, famous friends, and authority for living pushed upon us by our cultures will bring joy.

I felt in a safe place as the first person I met, said, "Pastor Jim, nobody can hurt you here." I am not a medical doctor. I do trust that soul healing requires medication and cognitive change. My healers believed that the commodity that strengthens our innermost being is the joy of the Lord. That joy empowers us to become the person God thought of when thinking of each human on the journey.

Joy is not insipid, weak, and rapidly changing emotion. Joy heals us best when we are experiencing the worst. Read Proverbs 17:22. In the ancient Hebrew language, joy is translated as "expressing joy or rejoicing." Read Psalm 126:5-6.

Farmers have a love for the land. They enjoy the produce that comes. Our family owns a farm in Nebraska. Joy comes as farmers dig in the dirt, plant seeds in the tender ground in the spring season, pulling weeds under the hot sun. They harvest the bounty in the fall. In the garden of God as you may sow in tears, you will reap in joy.

One of my psychiatrists told me that being hospitalized was the best thing for me. He noted that those patients who have sown tears of sadness, disappointment, and hopelessness have the greatest capacity to reap a life filled with the joy from heaven.

Doing the ministering of God, Paul and Silas were beaten by angry citizens. They were bruised and bleeding. Clothes were torn from bodies. They were in need of medical attention.

They were not brought to a healing place like Deaconess Hospital, but they were tossed into a Roman prison. Their feet were locked in stocks.

A Roman prison was a place of nearly instant mental illness. Prisoners would lose their minds after a few days in the black fetid place. Prisons were built in the belly of the earth. They reeked of vomit and urine. Only one meal was allowed. Each day they received moldy bread with some dirty water that had been used for other unmentionable things.

They had to sit in excrement with mice and insects crawling over their bodies. These men must have been given tremendous cognitive therapy by the Great Physician. Acts tells us they actually sang songs of joy in that worst of places.

God was rejoicing over me and the other patients. God was singing. Despite the atmosphere of a fallen world, joy is found. We played a lot of pool and ping pong as we shared together. We read James 1:2-4. Only in a Christian hospital would patients seriously seek joy. Ministers of God are not immune to depression.

Most patients came with broken hearts. They grappled with life's plight in a differing way than those who were unbelievers. They were too numb to think well. This side of heaven there are events, circumstances, people, and issues that breaks human hearts.

One day as I could sense that I was healing, I asked God to make me an expert on joy. Depression had weakened me. Joy would strengthen me. Depression cuts off the source of life. Joy fertilizes abundant life.

In group therapy sessions, we heard words of bitterness and blame. Some numbed themselves by watching television. Refusing participation in therapeutic activities brought on ravenous emotional appetites. We all gained weight as the hospital provided delicious pleasuring fruit, filling meals, and we could eat any time.

Walking with God helps us act, look, talk, and feel, the opposite of natural tendencies or human genetic pre-disposition. Through any trial or illness, people tend to rant and rave, complain and whine. Those who were healed had inner attitudes in every future circumstance.

The doctors reminded us that there will be, after we go home, situations in life will again cause us to choose things that cause more unhappiness. Keeping company with cheerful believers finds no mirth like those who walk others home.

My experience has given me a vertical perspective with the spirit of God living inside. Those who hold on to a horizontal point of view will keep on gazing at a barren wasteland. The choice is ours.

If we choose to live a life of compromise. And selfishness and still be a beneficiary of the joy of heaven, we have chosen wrongly. I can share with you from personal experience, we cannot have sin and joy simultaneously. We must determine to demolish momentary pleasures in order to be blessed with joy.

When joy is restored into our lives, we make a difference during earthly journeys. God needs a generation of joyful people to take on the problems of this world.

Like most depressed people, I felt guilt. Some choices caused me to believe if I could not be the best, then I was worthless. Therapists insisted I not use words like should, ought, or must. Something kept me saying those words and to rephrase what I had been saying in positive thinking and a feeling of contentment. I gained the insight that my guilt was harmful and that it came from teachers, parents and ministers imposed on me since childhood. Guilt accused me of being a bad person, causing me to hide what I had done. I hated the anger and disapproval of powerful people from the past. My fear was that they would not love me. I could not love myself because I did not meet their standards. Guilt had an unprofitable bedfellow called shame that would keep anybody from loving me.

Despite my stinking thinking, the guilt and shame paralyzed me. I felt remorse. Remorse is a healthy sadness. We experience it when we have hurt or offended another. We think that we have failed to live up to the best that we can be.

I began to see my wounds in a better light. I saw a brighter future. I did not realize just how disabling my wounds were. How would I function differently if God led me to accept another call as a spiritual leader or pastor.

After moving to our new home in Saint Joseph, Missouri, God presented me with a call to be the pastor for Pilgrim Presbyterian Church in Cameron where I experienced ten happy years of service. God miraculously has a ministry for those God calls.

Joyless religion is dangerous.

A sign of losing joy in life is living without joy. Joy is a vital gauge on the dashboard of life. When the needle dips we know by life and death canaries. Coal miners know that dangerous gases gather silently in the tunnels. Carbon monoxide will asphyxiate them. Methane explodes.

In early times of coal mining, they discovered a low-tech solution. They brought canaries into the mines. A canary's metabolism is sensitive to air quality. These yellow birds chirp and sing to indicate the air is safe. When gas levels rise, the birds stop singing. Wobbling on their perch, they fall to the floor of their cage.

Genuine joy is like that singing yellow bird. One of the effects of sin is the loss of joy. When our hearts stop singing, that is a warning to us. Do not confuse unique joy with other upbeat feelings. Joy is not only the power of positive thinking. Joy is not a bubbly, optimistic personality. Joy is not walking through life with a naïve, glass-half-full attitude.

Joy is the emotion of salvation. We cannot produce joy ourselves. Joy is a glorious gladness with deep delight. Joy is never extinguished by circumstances of tough seasons. Read Habakkuk 3:17-18. As a barometer, joy is not a slave to circumstances.

Joyless Faith Is No Faith.

The epidemic of joyless faith is missing out. My grandson Ethan gave a moving speech on Youth Sunday at Bradley Hills Presbyterian Church. He spoke about how his church has supported, guided, and created guidance. From personal experience, I grasp the truth. Experiencing lack of joy and the elusions of joy. As you read this book, the reader deals with the part joylessness plays. God has promised to give joy. The joy of the Lord is real strength. Divine joy is not fabricated happiness. Joy is not just a temporary feeling. Gathering with believers is the place love and peace mix with joy? Read II Thessalonians 1:16-17.

Scripture tells us it is in the house of God. Meeting with God's people in prayer, knowing the love, dealing with problems, and being in God's family is the source of joy. Walking each other home is unhurried. A joyful congregation is a slice of heaven.

During my ministries, we have felt that something will happen. It does. Through the years, I have experienced many people arriving at worship with obvious feelings of joy with eager anticipation. They met the living Christ. The Spirit of God filled them. That spirit filled New Testament Christians. No Bible, just oral tradition, told them about Jesus. They passed the stories to each other.

Joyless Christianity misses out. Hit the reset button if a church becomes a church centered on anxiety, anger, guilt and fear. The Spirit of Joy Church is where God is pleased. We are living as we were designed. Few live in a family to live a focused life. Narrow is the way. Few find it. The spiritual joy transcends struggles and difficulties. Living for oneself is futile. The sacrifice of our small, insignificant selves can make the vital difference in someone else. God has led me to realize that joy is not present in the walk with the Creator, there is a misunderstanding of faith. Not just pleasure, fleeting emotion, but joy.

Smiling and singing enthusiastically is not joy. Never allowing spiritual highs, we never risk being brought low. A sour, non-exulting demeanor has a deadening effect that drags others down. With a lack of love, we will turn others away from the gospel. Get up from special-needs chairs. Ignite the fire of joy under others who continue sitting in the joyless places. That chair is one of weakness. Having a religious experience is not seeing the "Light of the knowledge of the glory of God in the face of Christ." Read II Corinthians 4:6. The joy of infancy is precious. When we first know God, we are immature in faith. Prolonged immaturity squelches joy. Elizabeth Elliot noted, "The recognition of who God is a life-long process."

Sustained joy is impossible without obeying. Disobedience kills motivation, fellowship, prayer, and disciplines that are essential in pursuing joy. The natural outcome of the Christian's obedience to the will of God is joy. Read Psalm 16:11.

God desires us to be joyful. Joyless relationships fall apart. They just don't work. Churches will sacrifice the joy of being in intimate relationship with God for cold, dead practices. Joy-filled churches live in the understanding that when coming out on the other side of trials brings more joy than can be comprehended.

Joyless people have no respect for others. Abiding joy causes awareness of God's grace. Joy results from demonstrating grace in relationships.

Joyless religionists focus on issues rathe than the Issuer. God is faithful to know needs. Seek God first, not the needs. Read Matthew 6:33.

Joy protects us from cultural religion. Joy keeps us safe as we serve. If there is no joy, our work for God is no longer worship. We find we are serving God for the wrong reasons. Joy keeps us safe from serving as a religious duty.

Awareness of joy keeps us from temptation. When we get up from the table after a Thanksgiving meal, the last thing I desire is more food. Even the best dessert does not tempt me.

To illustrate the concept of joy, my dear Nebraska friend Mae Grill says she would "hug you and laugh looking into your eyes with love and what we share would show us how joy looks." Joy is when we feel connected to others and love unconditionally. In a joy we feel safe. We know who we are. We are grateful for how blessed we are. We remember in our hectic seasons and stressful world to connect with joy.

Transformation and joy are available to anyone. Age or background, in season or out, we can ignite our incredible potential. Pray and work to discover it, to shape it, to forge it in the fires of life, and share it with the world.

Albert Schweitzer said, "By having a reverence for life, we enter into a spiritual relation with the world. By practicing reverence for life, we become good, deep, and alive." Those who survive cancer, bad marriages, horrid jobs ignite a new perspective. There is a new reverence for life. They enjoy every moment.

Losing joy is losing strength. Joy is essential. Joy is always a possibility. Scripture commands rejoicing. "Rejoice with me." Read Luke 15:6,9. "Rejoice … your reward is great in heaven." Matthew 5:12. "Leap for joy." Luke 6:23. Joy in the soul of a creature intertwines with the gifts of the Creator. Joylessness equates with emotional inconsistence and spiritual dullness.

Thanksgiving bestows reverence. Joy gives everyday epiphanies. Children find joy in situations where parents are upset and irked. A child experiences everything with awe, wonder, and joy. Spirits and souls can create joyful lives by merging and connecting to God. Becoming like a child, God becomes our parent. We have a limitless capacity for doing what we were designed to do. Schweitzer was a missionary of joy for years in Africa. After serving with gifts of music, of medical expertise, of preaching, and teaching, he wrote, "He who loses his reverence for any part of his life will lose reverence for all of his life."

On your walk home each night, find an unwinding vision quest. If you drive home, before you start your automobile, write a to-do list for the next day. Come home with presence, free from personal burdens.

Augustine said, "May the live coal of joy grow hot within my spirit and break forth into a perfect fire; may it burn incessantly on the altar of my heart. May it blaze in the recesses of my soul."

Some modern mystics will not accept a definition of joy, when the atmosphere quivers, vibrating within. In the Bible, angels and humans broke out into other-worldly joy. It was grand and pervading. They experienced joy as a wave of splendor. All is well, always has been, and always will be.

Wesley expressed his joy of salvation as "my heart was strangely moved." An Indian Christian described it as an endless smile. That smoldering joy was an infinite ocean of eternal love broke on the calm endless shores of my soul. Blissful joy, the nectar of immortality pulses through like quicksilver fluidity.

God is committed to give eternal joy. Joy is tied to the glory of God. God is not indifferent to Divine glory. External circumstances in a fallen world can bring brief pleasure. That pleasure is empty, thin, and frivolous.

Joy runs deeper and wider than joylessness. Deep and enduring joy is a gift from God. Joy as gladness and delight is no better than an erratic inconstant lover. Somewhere inside us we know we are meant for joy. We feel the bitterness between desire and disappointment. Secular and false images keep us wanting more. We are blindly attempting the impossible.

Writing a book sometimes makes prayer time almost impossible. She can't stop thinking about what she is going to write. And sometimes the whole book needs revising.

In those confusing times, I stop. I ask God to guide my fingers as I attempt to write what God would write. Prayer is part of creation. When I pray in public or preach a sermon, I always ask God to give me freedom by guiding my communication to just what God desires to say. Sometimes without thinking of it, an illustration hops into my mind, and someone will say, "When you gave that example, I finally knew what love God has for me." Writing means striking out words or whole paragraphs or entire chapters.

The biblical and spiritual descriptions are minimized. These are missing in religious teaching in favor of ideological interpretation or reductionism of science. In the 50 years that I have shared my joy and the joy of others walking me home to eternal joy, I observed churches and ministers removing religious experiences from religion and the spirit from spirituality. Expressions of joy have been suppressed in both the academic study of joy, and in the recent practice of faith. We can't define or get an accurate picture of our final calling. Nobody has the eye of God. Our souls are eternal. Souls will never cease to exist. They are tuned in to the frequency of God. Human souls are like an AM radio. They pick up stations, but they cannot get FM signals.

That what Jesus was trying to teach Nicodemus. If one is not made alive in the spirit, she cannot see the things of the Spirit.

Jesus told the woman at the well that God is Spirit. Anyone who approaches God must do so in truth and spirit. Jesus pointed to the spirit dimension. It is impossible to access on our own no matter how sincere or religious they are.

During his life journey, Jesus told some people that they could not go where he was going. To some others, he promised he was going to prepare a place for them to be forever with him. The difference was the condition of their spirits.

Hell-bent, self-righteous, and culturally proud people trivialize and pathologize any ecstatic experience evaluating them of being of ignorance, fanaticism, and superstition.

In spite of attempts to quash it, misunderstood joy has continued to be awakened, healed, renewed, nurtured, excited, and totally remade diverse seekers in Christian history in every nation on earth.

My calling as Minister of Joy to the World is an obsession, a source of endurance and manic energy. Experiences of joy are mysterious clusters of energy deep in the unconscious charged by mysterious moments. We spend our lifetime trying to recapture all that brought into ecstasy and obsessive interest. The feeling is like coming home to do something special. Do the things that I write in this book and the spirit of joy will fill your life.

Smiles radiating from a joyful heart, especially from a child as eyes sparkle, makes the body radiate in its awesomeness.

Rare experiences cannot be kept at bay. We have come to be too fearful of and embarrassed by embodied emotion and devotion. Ignore demeaning talk and enjoy the higher fire of God that burns beyond cold-hearted naming and shaming. Growing Pentecostal denominations would still be part of mainlines and traditional churches if people were not so afraid of emotional expressions. We stiff believers desire to be spiritually cooked by new waves of feeling. That desire puts you in good immortal company. Pray with the steam and longing dream of Saint Augustine. Spirit of Joy congregations pray like that.

Praying that someone be restored, healed, or death deferred causes wonder about those who Jesus raised from death. Jairus's daughter, the widow's son, Lazarus, all died a second time. They probably worried about what the second dying would be like?

Heaven is our home. Homecoming was made possible ever since death became the reality in the garden of Eden. God made home on earth. Jesus' home was in a small village in a place that was occupied by the Roman empire. His estrangement from home was a price for human homecomings. Homesickness is human life in momentary affliction. Home becomes forever joy.

Jesus is joyously in love with each one. Nothing we do would be a reason to defer his love in the prevailing and magnificent way only God can give. Jesus' love is stronger than any rejection, every failure, every hurt, and every worry.

Joy is the most reliable evidence of the presence of God. That's why joy is utterly important. We must share it. Joy is the most vital sign of connection. The well from which we draw joy is often filled with tears. I am so thankful for this book. Its roots are in 70 years as a minister. Life Forces us to be pragmatic. The ultimate reason for human inquiry is not this life but the afterlife. Culture perceive itself as educationally and technologically advanced.

People are aware of eternal significance, but do not pursue it. The pastoral and personal make this writing a double joy.

Joy is experienced to be shared.

When my grandson Ethan was born, I phoned our family members and closest friends to share the joy. The shared joy caused us to bubble all over. Joy is meant to be shared. That's why I write so many books on joy. It is my purpose to preach joy, teach joy, pray joy, paint joy, and let God use my life for this reason. Joy becomes more complete when we share it with others. The moment I first saw Ethan was placed in the videos of my joys. Having others to share our joys brings even more excitement. Sharing new things with others improves their lives. It allows them to discover the same joy. Sharing joy makes our own joys complete. Joy brings flourishing seasons that are unselfish on every level to invite others to experience the same.

That's how joy is cultivated. Not by working at the highest intensity, getting recognition and honors, becoming well-known, but in the ordinary moments. Watch the videos of our memories of joy times. And watch how he move with angry thoughts. We become resentful. I am not writing to tell you that you will never be angry. We are human. We cannot avoid being angry. We can avoid cultivating it.

The ability to feel joyful does not come from favorable circumstances. It comes from God with limitless wisdom. We cannot lose joy any more than losing God.

The spring season begins an eternal presence. The love of God lasts forever. The joy found in God is not a static emotion. Joy regenerates us. There is no lasting power except God.

The foundation is unshakable awareness that we know love. Joy is the beginning of the kingdom of God. Nothing can take away the knowledge and wisdom coming from God. God, or stop you from "the joy of the Lord."

Prayer puts us in touch with the power of God that frees us from fear. We feel safe and the healing power of joy transforms us. We do not ever have to feel desperate concerning and problem. Read Isaiah 35:10.Joy is shared in "a million different ways," an expression from a new television program about life in all seasons.

Communicating and sharing the love and joy from God, I have used preaching, teaching, painting, and psychotherapy. I had planned to invite my readers to join sessions of my "soul healing" or psychotherapy from the Greek words for "soul" and "healing." I have hundreds of books from which how I have conducted counseling as a psychiatric therapist. I am a licensed mental health practitioner in Tennessee and. Nebraska. I am now a trained and certified life coach.

Each credential has helped me be a source for helping people find joy in every season. I am a chartered member of the American Association of Christian Counselors.

Each encounter with others has been unique to the problem or issue that a person brings. I am not going to share that as I am not a model for any professional except as an ordained minister of joy to the world.

A cherished book is *Christ Centered Therapy: The Practical Integration of Theology and Psychology* written by Neil Anderson and Terry and Julianne Zuehlke. I bought the 431- page book for $25 from Zondervan in 2000.

The purpose of this book is to show how to integrate Christ-centered counseling with the requirements of managed care and professional psychology. This book addresses the needs of the whole person. This volume provides balanced options for clients to find wholeness and resolution.

The book has been called a gold mine for detailed and specific help for any pastor, counselor, or seeker who allows Christ into their practice. The authors give samples of treatment plans, legal documents for people to sign, using the contributions of science as powerful resources to help in understanding soul-healing.

The first section equips us with an understanding of the different issues involved in integrating theology and psychology. I advise most ministers not to attempt to do counseling. The risk is too great.

The second section helps turn theory into practical application. The authors challenge us to avoid the troubles and problems that are more and more apparent in legal, health related, and spiritual areas.

The authors give in the appendix personal testimonies. They provide professional forms, discuss the role of psychiatry in managed care.

Intercessory Prayer for Joy

Loving God, I thank You for the joy and peace that I have in my trust. Today, I lift my brothers and sisters in Christ who are going through difficult times or feeling alone or discouraged.

Holy God, who comes in an hour, in a way I lest expect, in ways I cannot predict. Deliver me from falseness and deception. Save me from the pride that demands exception, the worry that negates faith, the depression that clouds options, jealousy that destroys character, affluence that forgets poverty, hatred that destroys relationships, envy that ruins life, and selfishness that usurps rights of others

Mysterious God, I pray that love and joy will fill their hearts. Flood our inner beings with overflowing by the power of the Spirit.

My soul longs for guidance as earthly visions dim my perspective. Keeping commandments brings joy. Give purpose to my seeking heart. Bestow heaven-oriented vision to my weary eyes. Let my hands do good work. Set my feet to walk in righteousness. Set my mind on Thy thoughts. May I not falter. May I never forsake faith. Keep me and use me.

Help each one walk home together with deeper dependence and in closer communion. May be possess a peace and joy that passes all understanding. Guard their souls and that they may find heaven-sent joy. In Jesus' name. Amen.

Practical Application

Draw a line horizontally across the middle of a page. At the extreme left side write the word "birth." With five-year intervals, on the top part of the line, write the "hills," or positive events. On the bottom write the word "valleys" and list negative things such as troubles.

Understand that every action you take and every word you say will have an effect on all the world around you.

SUMMER

"Everything in life, indeed everything in history, converges on Jesus Christ and radiates from him bringing fulfillment of joy in everything."

--Nicholas Wolterstorff

God is never far from us in summer. We see God's handiwork in nature. Rainbows remind us of a long-kept vow. Harvests speak of promised blessings. Pausing at the zenith of nature's magnificent glory, we pray for believing to our intimate God. In summertime the blessings of the good earth merge with growing faith into a benediction of grace.

Listen to favorite summer songs. Music evokes joy. Sleep under the stars. Camping trips give nature fixes. Enjoy free days with permission to switch off. Body, mind, and soul will thank you.

Launch new things. Squirreling away behind the scenes gets us pleasantly stuck into new stuff.

During the summer season, joyful people smile a little more brightly. If blue skies and joy vibes have not crept their way into your soul yet, do not worry. Joy is as a butterfly. When we pursue one, it is beyond grasp. Just sit still and it might surprise us by landing on our shirt.

Without air conditioning in our Bristol home, summer had its downsides. I still remember those breathless nights when my father prowled the house in the wee hours of a summer evening looking for some relief from the heat. Worse was my mother's litany, "You boys go outside and get some fresh air."

Why go out in the sun, sweat, and get a headache when it was so much nicer to sit next to the fan and read? Summer brought an overabundance of stinging insects and smothering heat.

Summer is a time to rejoice. Sometimes things like the pandemic, illness, uncertain careers, broken relationships, fears, divorce, and death knock the wind out of us. Hearts are broken. Souls are battered. We walk each other home as the walking wounded. Shake off binding chains. Go forward. Run with intention, hope, and purpose.

Step out of the rut of sadness. Energize out of numbness. Blame less. Bless more. Hate less. Love more. Doubt less. Dream more. Gripe less. Cheer more. Sit less. Move more. Discourage less. Encourage more. Feel the joy return. Getting confused and lost is easy. Trapped, we wish our lives away. Starting becomes difficult. Focus on what God is saying.

Still, we refuse to believe that summertime has ended. We wish the season would go on forever. It is as startling when our own leaves begin to change. Our favorite season comes and goes in every year. We must dance with each season. Pain and suffering, misery and unhappiness are the result of trying to paddle upstream against the current of life. There is no joy in attaching to a particular season.

One of my vision quests involved brainstorming during a joy making conference called "Creating a Sacred Summer." We were so excited. We shared memories of summers past. We talked about how special things like finding shells on a beach. We were ecstatic at all the broad array of summer symbols that gained spiritual significance when we zeroed thoughts and joyful feelings. Spontaneous summer spirituality stirs senses to draw us closer the God.

Summer experiences stir the senses and introduce spiritual practices that add meaning in ways that are not always obvious. Giving ourselves time to retreat and listen, learn, and recreate forming tools that yields a special summer.

We are especially hungry during these pandemic days for intimate times with God. Refueling is needed now. God converts all seasonal symbols into spiritual joy.

Refueling is to spiritually reenergize. My anointing mentor, Norman Vincent Peale, said, "The more you lose yourself in something bigger than yourself, the more energy you will have."

Tap into the energizing bunny to find spiritual renewal. It is located inside not outside. Spending time with children brings new energy. I go home physically tired, but spiritually energized when I encounter a child. Meditation, contemplation, silence seeps into the soul. Focus on breathing. Feel each breath flowing in and out from your heart. We call our annual men's retreat a recharge. Slowing down and feeling presence with God recharges me. Take time to experience the resting in your soul and renewal of spirit. Stress zaps energy. Constant pressure is exhausting. Deep breathing helps. Avoid rushing. Wake up early. Walk out of the path of energy suckers. Limit time and exposure to energy takers. Counteract that time by hanging wit energy givers. Make home a haven for experiencing the joy of energy givers. Give no invitations for energy zappers.

There are no perfect summer moments. Life never turns out as we envision. We plan for a vacation or some time to be in a pleasant setting, but life happens.

Again, I find renewed joy in the positive language of Norman Peale: "You only lose energy when life becomes dull in your mind." Energy is a sign of inner wellness. Souls vibrate in the love of God. Feeling drained and exhausted requires doing something fun. A positive enthusiastic spirit affects vitality recharging with light and life forces. Explore what robs you of energy.

Circumstance is that circle we are standing in. We are never standing still. When a seeker painstakingly reviews, repeats, stays stuck because of circumstances, they force themselves to be hurt even more. We can tell of our current troubles. God wants us to seek answers. Joy comes back when we rise about our circumstances. If it is a chronic but brief circumstance, we must change our perspective.

Take responsibility for your circumstances. Do not possess what you want to release. Yes, the circumstances belong to us. Give those circumstances to God. God is bigger than your current trouble. Our worries, cares, concerns, deepest affliction, depression must be cast toward a healing God. My mom used to say, "Don't tell God that you have a big problem. Tell your problem that you have a big God." Read Isaiah 55:8-9. Bringing God down to our level invites disaster. Many occasions than we could number, we hear troubled people ask, "Why God? Why me?" We need to let God be God. That is the only way humans will not be defeated, deluded, deceived, or destroyed by circumstances people can use against us. Charles Spurgeon said, "If we cannot believe God when circumstances seem to be against us, we do not believe God at all." Albert Einstein advised, "We cannot solve problems with the same thinking we used when we created them."

The wisdom and thinking of the world will not help. Humans are prone to be impatient. Believe that God has heard your prayers. The answer is on its way. It might be delayed, but it has not been denied. The world changes. Circumstances will change. God's intimate Word will never change.

Cloistered in our homes, we zoom into online church, make appearances in other people's videos and blobs. We allow the pandemic to do its work. I sit by the fireplace, and think about what I have said and done.

I slept until my body was rested. I walked in the morning sunlight. The pace intensified the sense of being who I am. I retired from church supported employment. Sitting alone in the quiet, the voice inside of me became discernible and clear.

I came to realize that by realizing blessings in the past, by actualizing opportunities in the present, and by anticipating the glorious transformation coming in the future.

A historian was asked by a student to summarize human history in as few words as possible. Expecting an academic response, the student and the class awaited the response.

The teacher spoke and he amazed the students in the room by simply saying, "They were born. They lived. Finally, they died."

That is what we read on grave markers when we visit a cemetery. We see a birth date, a dash, and a death date. What is inscribed on tombstones a similar summation of one's life. We live in anticipation of our transformation promised future.

If I have any influence on those who bury me, I want the words on my burial marker to read, "Minister of Joy to the World."

Dealing with difficult circumstances is a given if you are still breathing. Circumstances are temporary. God is eternal. Circumstance will not limit your blessing. We need not fear any circumstance because God can work for good in any circumstance. Read II Corinthians 9:8. God will give us favor and abundant blessing in whatever circumstance we face. No matter what our troubles are, we can find a reason to be grateful.

We can thrive under pressure. Gifted and loving people want to leave a legacy, by a life that makes an impact. Most of us live an unknown but faithful life in small places. Read I Timothy 2:2-4 and I Thessalonians 4:11-12. An honored life is one that is peaceful and quiet. Such a life journey leaves a pleasant fragrance. The world thinks that sounds obscure, behind-the-scenes life. We are rarely encouraged to lead quiet lives because we think a quiet humble life has no impact. God's will for us might just be one not involving numbers, followers, gaudy statistics, and awards.

Joy is tinged with frustration with unexpected upsets. We experience accidents. A loved one gets sick or dies. Unexpected upsets always surprise us. These major frustrations include the outside world with a pandemic, catastrophic fires, tornadoes and floods. We are in a healing energy atmosphere.

Summer invites moments of lingering with sunsets. We enjoy the smell of barbecue. Summer allows reset buttons. Our hot button of joy helps us find our way back to a better feeling place. The roses in the garden burst with fragrance. Summer invites us take time to smell the flowers.

Summer directs us for opportunities for outdoor get togethers, to catch up with friends and family with a picnic or barbecue. We notice the longer days of sunlight. There is more warmth than in any other season.

God never takes a vacation. God is with us in all seasons. Continue to enter summertime in grace and the power of now.

In my church in Weeping Water, I preached a long series on spirituality and sexuality one summer. New young adult members viewed the topic as vital. Church doors opened. We spread our arms wide to welcome people to step inside. Most of them navigated the joy and sorrow outside the walls of the church. Our vision was helped with 12 special small groups on substance abuse, mental health, coping of older adults, a youth group for youth who were avoided, and other connections to their daily life.

Ministry happens in secular and sacred places. People need help navigating attitudes toward sexuality that they encounter every day. Most churches remain silent. They remain disconnected. Faith communities that listen and respond to joys and troubles have a chance to survive and thrive.

Jesus went out into the secular world. He sent others out. Going out from Jerusalem, his leadership connected to the people he encountered. The marketplace, the seashore, the town pool, at weddings, and in homes. Read the gospel's accounts. Notice that Jesus taught about simple so-called secular things: wines and branches, seed, sheep, salt, bread, and mustard seeds.

Church leaders show up in social and political meetings. School board meetings, zoning, tending a city park, food banks, or health issues find people of faith. There is no secular world. God so loved all the world. Leaders walk into the community sharing life and concerns as Jesus did. People who never "darken the doors of church" experience joys. Thriving congregations never use the term "us and them," but walking with each other is the mission. Go to the outsider. Speak to needs. Encounter the needy. Be Christ to those we choose to walk with faith.

Pray in your own special way for the housebound, for those who cannot go out or enjoy a barbecue, for those in hospice, for the homeless and those in prison.

Limiting factors determine the quality of living in every season. Saying life is busy and the schedule is full is an understatement.

Thank God you are busy. In all my years of research on joy, I have not had one person who did not practice gratitude. Practicing thanks invites joy. The practice of joy changed my life. I have scores of gratitude journals. After saying grace at a family meal, we share something for which we are grateful.

This ordinary experience invites more joy into the home. Joy causes gratitude. Gratitude makes us joyful.

Think gratitude. Daymond John said, "We are what we think about. I believe the last think I read at night will manifest when I am sleeping. We are what we think about the most."

Life is not a 100-yard dash, but a marathon.

My brother Dr. Edward W. McReynolds, M.D. is a doctor of the body. He was recently honored for 50-years as a physician in Wilmington, Delaware. In his office, Dr. Ed displayed his medals from completion of marathons and iron man races throughout the United States and Canada.

He graduated from the University of Tennessee Medical School, where he met his Sherry. Wife Sherry and his family including daughters Wendy and Holly traveled with him.

Ed participated in many challenges including the iron man in Hawaii and other places. During the Boston Marathon, the heat rose into the 90s. Many runners dropped out with leg cramps, heat strokes, or dehydration. Sometimes he would "hit the wall," as runners, something runners dread. He was exhausted. His legs felt like lead. Shooting pains rose from his feet. Marathoners want to quit, but most keep running to the finish line at 26.2 miles.

Runners absorbed empathy and hope from a crowd of half a million people lining the streets of Boston. Clapping and shouting, they would yell, "You are doing great. You can finish."

In running the race of life, all of us "hit the wall," where pain, exhaustion, grief, doubt, discouragement, aloneness, or spiritual dryness block progress in the journey.

In Ed's race, the support of his family and the cheering of the crowd helped him finish the race. We need fresh glasses of living water for souls to run the race of life.

It is normal for people to encounter "the wall." That assurance enabled us to resist self-judging and shaming in our trials. We are renewed in deeper grace with intimacy with God.

"The wall" insists that the weight we carry is not serving us. Let go. Move forward. Let go of comparison. Comparison is a thief of joy. Impossible ideals and achievements by others cause frustration. Authentic lives are not consumed by what others are doing. Let go of comparison. It is more difficult to be envious of others when you bask in appreciation for your life.

Forgive me when I lower standards with weak resolve and mixed motives. Give me courage to rectify and the strength to overcome.

Let go of self-sabotage. Overscheduling or the "should and could" words. Some goals no longer serve our purpose. Whatever it is, unless it seriously lights our inside life, get it off your list. Open up more energy for goals that set us on fire. Fiery summers are exciting. Endless summers scorch earth. Heat warms. Letting go is difficult. Cooling off and chilling out are the gifts of the fall and winter seasons.

Pencil in time for quiet evenings at home. Wander around the neighborhood without other commitments. Breathe and relax. Remove the pressure. Surprises and curveballs arrive. Storms swirl around and rage within us. Seasons bring strength, weakness, heartache, and joy. Our relationship with God is tested. Immense changes come. Remain rooted in faith. Summertime is legacy-making time.

Our faith is shaken by rough winds of circumstances. Feeling anxiety and stress will not uproot us. Grace is sufficient. Read Psalm 143:8. When roots are shallow, we feel chocked by the thorns of life. Root firmly in the storm. Remain rooted in the Spirit in every season. Go together across the road and over the bridge.

Prayer for Joy in Work

Dear loving God. I am grateful for my job and for those who walk with me. Thanks for helping me provide for my family.

Be close to families where a child lies sick or handicapped as sadness pervades the home.

Be close to families where a parent is sick or missing and bills go unpaid.

Be close to families who are always in crises, where confused communication and emotional instability lead to hatred, feuding, jealousy, and where everyone loses.

Guard and keep my loved ones safe. May those who gather in the home forgive each other when they are wrong. Lead us to be reality oriented, evaluating our motives.

Lord, I want to carry out my work each day to honor You. Continue to provide me with strength, wisdom, and grace to fill my many tasks and duties. May I finish each responsibility with an inner peace and a joyful disposition.

God, thank you that the joy of the Lord is my strength. I pray that work colleagues and every person I encounter that they may see the love of Jesus flowing through me. May each choose the desire to have that joy of knowing him. I confess sins that become a barrier to joy: malicious thoughts, hasty conclusions, undisciplined habits, half trust, conditioned love, unguarded criticism, unrepented greed, wavering faith, and evil deeds.

Allow me to be more like Jesus through whom I confess my sins. Amen.

Practical Application

Spend a few minutes in prayer for someone else. Keep a prayer journal and write down others' needs and requests.

Write someone a thank you note or email about your appreciation or the role they played in your life.

List three more things you are thankful for today.

Make the following declaration: "I declare today that I will express joy regardless of my circumstances. I will not allow the pain of my past or disappointment influence my levels of joy. "

FALL

"Jesus says yes to his Father's creation and goes in search of all beings lost in the world's maze, in order to bring them home."

--Hans von Balthasar

Fall

Fall brings the sensuous songs of September. Fall brings refreshing cool breezes and the expansive white cotton candy clouds in the infinite blue sky as we move into the time school starts. Change is everywhere as children advance to higher grade levels. The young grow up and we, when we grow wisdom, grow younger. As the song reminds us, "Try to remember that day in September and follow, follow, follow."

Joy of Music

Traveling the world with Diane Bish, brings amazing joy. She plays organs throughout Europe in massive cathedrals that are filmed for her television program called "The Joy of Music." Diane gives another seven-day tour on the 40th anniversary of her work. What an autumn thrill!

Music is the art of memory. Videos hang in our mind as we recall songs all our lives. Hymns heard in childhood are dear in every season. Residents with dementia in nursing homes light up with memories of hymns when these are shared. The joy of singing hymns and preaching in nursing homes triggers their past and they begin to sing the words.

Conscious decisions to use hymns from historical roots. Music is vital to church leadership. Music guides and nurtures spirits of joy. Reflecting on music senses the divine.

Music holds each of us together. Beauty happens in singing together. Choice of music appeals to hearts first. Musicians lead with intellect and emotion. Music inspires minds that inspire the world.

Where words leave off, music begins. Music never dies. Hans Christian Anderson said, "Where words fail, music speaks." Music, the universal language, is enjoyed in nations that cling to divisions. Music is the uniter despite divisions. Wine that fills cups of silence is music. Magical music opens doors that were tightly closed.

Embracing fall activities matches physical needs and sensations. Taking hikes amidst foliage and flowers, picking pumpkins, strolling through apple orchards, jumping in leaves, or decorating gourds connects to healing motion. Adjust sleep cycles. As the sun sets, prepare for rest.

Introduce natural seasonal scents to living spaces. Wild orange, cinnamon, cedarwood, ginger, sage, vanilla, and rosemary are pleasing fall smells.

Embrace for the perils of the surprising unknown. Each experience leads to wisdom. Experiencing the coronavirus pandemic has resulted in depression, illness, social protocols, fear, and death. Communicating online, working from home, quarantine, and reassessments are imaginative ways we cope. Seek the meaning of each season.

Each season teaches us lessons. Looking at nature, falling away happens in the fall. Leaves and the temperature change. God is calling for fall time to let things go. Nature provides examples. Let go. Problems of fall could ruin winter.

Fall is a reward for surviving the heat of summer. Fall is like spring again. Fall means color, especially the hues of autumn leaves. Fall is colored with baby-spanked pink, scarlet, crimson, orange, flame color, and red-purple color, which is my favorite. Autumn breezes bring a pleasant cool. The windows are thrown open again. Our bodies feel alive without the heat sapping energy. Fall has a distinct feel. Fall's aura comes on crisp, frosty mornings. Fall is a season for reflection. Fall gives a new perspective. Strolling along on the pathway, the foliage changes. Quietly God moves in our lives. Let the "joy of the Lord" encourage and strengthen the soul.

Fall begins earlier than we expect. Weeds and wild grasses appear to be curling up for winter. Stocks of corn stand tanning, browned, giving over to last things. The leaves of artistic trees give new definition to orange and scarlet.

Fall is alive with coppery colors dancing in sunlight. Shadings of red from watermelon pink to deep maroon shine in oak leaves. Yellow pales to a rich cream color. In Nebraska, thousands of cranes fly in perfect formation winging their way south. Farmers think what life would be like if crops fail, if rains did not come, if devastation covered the land.

Joy is a rare commodity. To rejoice is to know a deep sense of delight. Take time to allow the fragrances and aromas penetrate the deepest places in the soul. Pacing life brings intentionality. Presume each moment is pregnant with the presence of God. Without trusting joy, we come to discover that the script we have been handed in the play of life is not the part we thought we were trying out for. Accept that life is not under human control. Life brings changes, new arrivals and departures. Say yes to what we are given. Joy requires desire. If we receive gifts, we must get our hands out of our pockets. Ask God for the joy. Joy requires endurance. Joy is a paradox. Depth of suffering and the height of joy become involved. Facing the dark night allows us to see the dawning of joy. Joy is a mystery. I have learned more in the ordinary experiences and sharing joy with others than in all the academic endeavors.

In *The Book of Joy*, the Dalai Lama, Tenzin Gyatso, and Desmond Tutu, archbishop emeritus of South Africa invited the world to ask questions about joy. They collected more than a thousand in three days. The question that was most ask was how people could possibly live with joy in a world filled with so much suffering. (Dalai Lama and Desmond Tutu, *The Book of Joy*, p. 7)

These two spiritual leaders reminded us that how we choose to act each day is vital. The authors note that self-compassion is connected to self-acceptance. Having compassion for human frailties and vulnerability, are limits for all of us. We are most joyful when we focus on other folks, not ourselves. Bringing joy to others is the best way to experience joy. This requires courage as we feel the pain of others. In this way we experience so much more joy. Joy brings resilience and aliveness. (*Ibid.*, pp. 7, 261-262) The section on "Joy Practices" is amazing. (*Ibid*, pp. 308-348)

Recent times is a story without an ending. Shared experiences are stored in a waiting room absent of time. These make sense with dangers such as the pandemic and terrorism and uncertainty. Seasonal change creates space to rebalance. Purified space taps into body and mind. Sensory times are impressionable and impowering.

Small practices cleanse the mind. Fall alters perceptions. Fall fosters creativity. Autumn enhances joy and gratitude. Accept change without judgment. Fall themes of gratitude align minds with spirit. Stuck in a mundane cycle makes it hard to notice changing shifts. Running wild with the season connects to shifts in energy. Cutting ties with distraction recharges mental faculties.

Walking in the garden with God keeps us from obsessing on fear. Focusing on joy implies persistent, constant, concentrated effort.

Open eyes to the fear we project onto others. Do not accuse others to clear guilt. In anger distraction we speak too quickly. Distraction comes on friendly faces, lonely faces, uncertain faces, limitations, dilemmas, reversals, and disappointments. Look beneath the surface to distinguish the transitory from the eternal. Glancing below the surface, love has a chance.

Without sunlight, moonlight would have no contrast. Earth would dry up. Darkness would overwhelm. Flamboyant and spectacular life attract intense attention. The joy of the Lord keeps us from walking among starving cries, homeless pain, poor pleas. The soul cannot walk indifferently. Neither can we refuge to toil in the center of the pain of the world as we are illumined with heaven's light.

We never know when we will stumble on something that will be an inspiration for our next idea. Fall is the time for clarity, re-evaluation, and honesty as we focus on our callings and higher purposes. Each tangible, physical object in my private sanctuary holds a story about the content of when, where, how, and why. I have hundreds of pretty rocks from throughout the world with places and dates inked on each one.

A flood of memories with precious, delightful and sacred real-time, real-life, real place moments come to life when I declare one of these objects as sacred. Letting go of meaningful things is excruciating difficult. As I enter my 80s, my writing room is my private world of retreat. When I am alone, I am close to God. I need to be here with a favorite pen, in this inner chamber, my personal altar to all that is beautiful and true. Being in solitude is a necessary pleasure for painters and writers.

I know that I have a soulful space in my custom-built home awaiting my presence with my own energy, my own breath. I am always joyful with a pen in my hand, as a painter is with a brush dipping into fine pigment. When I am in my writing room, I am living in the present now moment. As I become invigorated by fall's temperatures. I am reminded of how much I enjoy my life's journey and all the love-filled souls who bring me so much joy.

Painting a little girl's fingernails with a rainbow of colors is pure joy. Erupting in laughter, she says it's so cool. Smiling never ceases as I enjoy days with my grandson. Joy involves spiritual discipline. Read James 1:2-4.

September never fails to bring joy as a turning of the wheel in the right direction. Fall brings an amazingly exhilarating adventure for living a loving, meaningful, and beautiful life. We are nostalgic and sentimental about the past seasons and who we were then. Every moment of these precious days holds the opportunity to shape our own destiny. In our souls, longings live and breathe and have their being. We are free to vigorously enjoy our work with passion.

The soul's autobiography is written in the joy of relationships. The fulfillment of loving and being loved and accepted for who we are at the core is fundamental.

Every preacher love bursting at the seems churches. Energy and enthusiasm ooze out. Fabulous music moves me. Buzzing with activity, people enjoy fellowship.

I love an empty church. God and me together. I need that silent time. Drawing back from the world helps us live fully in the world. I need to receive and give inspiration. Inspiration by the Holy Spirit stirs the soul. Spend time in a quiet church. Sing in a church choir. Read inspirational books. Allow the joy of God to fill you with power. Refocus on the invitation found in the word of God. Receive God's complete joy delivered by Jesus. Touch another. Gather in a small group.

Conscious touching involves the soul, the body, and the spirit. Love and passion come consciously and unconsciously. We are in the place we are meant to be. We experience exactly what is needed in soul development. Get fueled. Be fired up. Share the Good News.

In most challenging moments, with joy, our whole being communicates with us. We communicate with ourselves and other amazing souls. By listening we learn from the experiences of others.

Walk in the presence to change circumstances and fears, and these evaporate into nothingness. Walking with Jesus, we sidestep painful experiences.

Returning to Joy

After the trials during the pandemic, we are hungry for joy. Appetites for joy have increased. Spring brought a vaccine from Barney Graham, Drawing on his work at Vanderbilt Medical School, his work developed the covid-19 vaccine in record time. Like Jonas Salk's polio vaccine, it saved millions of lives. Returning to joy is natural as normal becomes real. A command and a promise, joy is the root of soulful longing. For some, joy appears out of reach. Human life is a vicious cycle of discontent and disappointment. Hundreds of seekers of joy keep telling people to "choose joy." That phrase gives insight, but it may lack the surrender of everything to God. Choosing joy is not easy. Joy never magically appears. For the garden to flourish, till new ground. Use this book as an internal dialogue. My joy in writing is my inner extrovert. Ask any writer with multitudes of ideas crashing into their minds.

We can choose habits that are most likely to build joy. Prayer is one of those habits. Prayer brings intimate peace leading to rejoicing. Read Philippians 4:4, 6-7.

Shelves of books on mindfulness and gratitude. Quieting by articulating feelings, focusing on constant thanks, prayer brings sweet intimacy and joy. Disappointment, not joy, results if we do not grow in prayer. Joy is relational. Paul's thesis is just that. His writing is deeply relational, personal, and communal. There is no joy unless we choose to walk each other home. One way to define joy is to know that someone else is glad to be with me.

Walk Among the World of People

Traveling the earth ignites clues to how people find joy. Finland is ranked number one as the happiest nation. As Wesley said, "The world is my pulpit." As I conversed with people who call home wherever they are living, I searched everywhere including the largest and richest countries. I found joy in remote places. Vanuatu,

Summer

Henry James said of summer, "Summer afternoons to me has been the most beautiful words in the English language." Indeed, summer is a time to enrich our souls through spending time in nature's miraculous beauty. Summertime is a season where we live by the rhythms of the sunrise and the sun fall. Days are longer with hours of shimmering sunshine. Summer knows when it has reached its peak. Summer evenings are a healing salve with lazy strolls into twilight. Add a little leisure to life. Summer makes soothing music. Paul wrote that God gives "all things" to enjoy. Read Romans 8:32 and I Timothy 6:17. Relaxed relationships spontaneously produce lasting memories. Celebrations for freedom flow on the fourth of July.

Contemplating God is a vesper of quiet meditation. We are diverted from our usual pace. Summer makes notice the warm relaxedness of earth. Like a healing salve on sunset evenings with lazy strolls into twilight, souls are drawn to contemplate. Memories are shaped in summer. Rainbows speak of a long-kept vow.

During the summer of 1962, my experiences in northern New Mexico brought into my soul a peace. The high desert is filled with pinon trees. These trees thrive despite the dryness. Living for centuries with little rain, heat in summer, frigid cold, storms, and wind. Unlikely places are where we discover them. Clinging to the side of a canyon, they are not protected. Roots go deep. Wrapping around big rocks, they endure the harsh landscape of the desert. Nurture a faith that struggles to put down roots. Wrap around ageless rocks of joy.

Find a home in calls to ministries. God's faithful servants live homeless in a sense. The journeys toward eternal homes are where they make their home.

composed of islands in the South Pacific, was a place flooded with smiles. Smiling activates joy. Smiling is a way of life in Vanuatu. Proud of their identity, culture, and traditions, people on the 83 islands of the archipelago speak 113 languages. Immediate and extended family is cherished. Embracing diversity and respecting all traditions. They discuss issues together.

Money is not emphasized. Ensuring that needs are met, they farm the land, and gather the sea and natural provisions. Life is simple. Life is difficult. Appreciating what they have—food, shelter, support, family, purpose, friendship, love and joy. Watching elders, the young people learn to tend the land. Knowing the limitations and boundaries, resources are preserved for grandchildren.

Despite the beauty of the islands, Vanuatu is vulnerable to natural disasters. Earthquakes, cyclones, and active volcanoes make it the riskiness capital of the earth. Acceptance of things they cannot control gives a peace.

World-embracing love can be experienced in every nation on earth. Christian mission fields are full of intriguing stories. As I traveled to places around the world, I learned about real mission work. Christian missionaries are dedicated women and men filled with love. Doctors and nurses work along with evangelists on most mission fields. Coming from the best medical schools, they spent their lives in backwater towns in struggling countries. Risking health and life, they serve in disease-infested parts of the world. That's the reason I received so many shots for my journeys. Dangerous, difficult, hot, cold, and loneliness, even death result. Full-time career missionaries will tell you without hesitation, "I do this out of my love for God and God's people."

Love lasts. Churches live and die. When all buildings are gone, love prevails. God's love is shed abroad through the Holy Spirit. Love captivates and spreads naturally. God never contains love. Love overflows. The joy of the Lord is ours to draw upon and share. In Jesus' death we receive eternal life.

When Feeling a Lack of Joy

Experiencing a lack of joy, we get much advice. Joy is the unknown that blocks a nobler life. Finding joy requires that we are open to learning effective ways of dealing with emotions. We have no direct control of feelings. God gives us power to make choices, free will, not directed by thoughts. God does not make us responsible for feelings.

Feelings are as changing as April weather in Nebraska. Feelings push and pull souls all over the place. That train runs on reason alone. Reason is our way to attempt to feel in control.

Feelings make wonderful servants, but horrible masters. Rarely feeling joy is a problem. The broken personality needs healing. To lack joy is to lack communion with God. Enjoying communion with God means practicing presence.

Blessings, greater than the mind can encompass, overflows with joy. Joy gives sustenance on perplexing days. Joy brings wisdom on needy days. Joy begats patience on harried days. Joy brings guidance on confusing days. Joy brings comfort in sad days. Blessings appear in all days. The watch care of God is with us every day.

A thunderstorm without rain is rare. The patter of raindrops will cool the air and relieve the overcharged atmosphere. Swollen brooks indicate snow will melt and a joy season is arriving.

These are step stones in the river of joy. Before reaching the shallows where stones, we wonder how we can cross the stream. When reaching one solid stone, we step on another. Joy is in the distance from the brookside.

Souls transform into a vibrant overflow as we learn to live in the spiritual reality of the river of life. Giving in to the feeling of a lack of joy is really selfish. This joylessness brings patterns of disregarding God. Our feelings are ruling us when we overeat, lose tempers, become impatient, isolate from people. The reason why feelings control is that we are not aware of them. Nothing is more important then giving significant time to being aware, verbalizing, and praying each day.

Becoming burned out in the fast-paced world is a common reason for lack of joy. Human beings must learn to shut the door against burden-bearing thoughts that come into our consciousness. Closing the door to selfish desires shall be replaced by the desires of God.

No one can produce joy. Joy is gift, a fruit of the Spirit. With joyful hearts we need no compromising convictions to find power. There is no joy in such an exchange. Fleeting pleasures are not a bargain for a soul. Choose to walk along the narrow paths of joy's devotion than the wide throughfares of worldly inducements.

Choosing Joy in a World of Joylessness

Lacking joy there lurks a spirit of joylessness. It comes with anger, anxiety, guilt, depression, and ingratitude. Downtrodden and lackluster portrayals are visible on faces hung in sorrow.

God intervenes in joyless lives. The basis of Christian joy is to know that God has always cared for the whole world. Incarnated in Jesus, we have a foundation for saving the soul.

Roman emperors staged bloody spectacles in the arena. Telemachus was in the audience viewing fights to the death with humans and animals. One day, Telemachus jumped onto the floor. He rushed between two gladiators. Shouting he cried, "In the name of God, stop. "A fighter cut him to pieces. That act stuck in the minds of many Romans. Telemachus was the last person to die for the amusement of Crowds. A bloodthirsty era ended. Knowing God intervenes give self-assurance.

Key to Knowing God's Joy

When we think of Christ's time on earth, he gave hallmarks for joy. Jesus gave his life for us. He demonstrated an unparalleled joy. Joy rests upon our faith. Bringing past into the present, we affirm our future. Eternity is yet to be. Joy is a building block. We experience joy. We don't analyze joy. Peaks of immense joy are not unique to Christians. Constant joy is pouring out as we walk each other home to heaven.

Mist, rain, cold, snow, and dark clouds brings joyless gloom. When the sun warms and enlightens spirits. Imagine a sunny mood despite the dark clouds. Joy remembers that clouds give rain and shade to water the inner and outer persona. Little breaks between the clouds expose a haven of little patches of sunlight.

Joylessness feels like a dark cloud. Life is dark and dreary stuffed with burdens that bring on hopelessness. The gloom limits the ability to see clearly or to understand the limiting pain. Joylessness comes from unclear thinking. Perceptions are inaccurate. My work as the minister of joy to the world is dedicated to eliminating the starvation for love and joy.

Mother Teresa is a model bring joy to everyone she met. She realized she by herself could not change the world. Serving Christ with every once of strength, she ministered against overwhelming odds.

Mother Teresa reached only a small percentage of the world's needy people. She taught that God never asks us to be successful, but to be faithful. Every day she said, "Thy will be done." Ministering under the wings of the care of God means we pray the model prayer.

Seven billion people are like seven billion living pieces of a jigsaw puzzle constantly changing. The will of God is best. Easy to say. Hard to believe. Unpleasant and disruptive circumstances were sources of complaints. Within God's will, there are no regrets.

Seeing clearly helps reframe stinking thinking.

Stinkers say, "I'm just not good at that." Joy helps us think, "How can I get better at my skill?" With my inward personality, writing has become more effective than my preaching. Turning me loose to write and I am ignited.

Not being good at anything means we need to practice strengths. Ignore weaknesses that are the weeds in the garden of the best self. Never waste time in lamentation of annoyances that distract.

Life's storms are huge, scary, and swirling. In Nebraska, thunderstorms appear out of nowhere. Heavy, consistent snow or rain sets in for days.

Joy is an act of the will. Earth is filled with melancholic beings. The sun returns following a storm. Always being changed and recovering from damage, gloom arrives with turbulent storms. In a world of pessimism, worry, fatalism, and catastrophe, the battle to claim joy is ongoing. Writing what we are thankful for at the end of a long day is uplifting. God is always listening infinitely and intimately. Nurturing gratitude boosts levels of joy with God's design for life.

Choosing joy supplants happiness. Intense experiences are not a spiritual barometer of where we are and where we are headed. Joy mingles inside when we suffer tragedy and disappointment. Life is fragile. Joy is an act of the will. Every morning, we work to choose cognitive patterns that reflect the truth that joy is in us. Joy is a choice of how we live. Joy comes as a consequence of discovering subtle signs that truth, goodness, and beauty exist all around us.

It is possible to change our negative habits and cultivate new ones. Mysterious joy comes out of a joyless heart when the soul surrenders to the kingdom of joy.

When I was at my lowest, I cried a deluge of tears. I stammered out, "I give up." Jesus came to earth to endure the pains we have. We experienced every emotion. He saw everything there was to see in the world. In joyless seasons, we need to be brought into joy. Hurt overwhelms us. We no longer see the light. We need God who has gone into the deepest depths. Bemoaning what we lose is useless. We find joy in all that remains.

The biggest tragedy is to become caught up in the complications of trying to change of fix joylessness. When lives come to the end of time, it will not matter how many years we have lived.

Accomplishments will be forgotten. We are mortal. Days of living are numbered. Appreciation for the simple, brief, and wonderful moment of joy creates lives worth living.

Knowing that our purpose, our calling, our job ignites sparks of enthusiasm. Making money and buying things cannot give any deep sense of fulfillment. Life satisfaction comes from using our gifts and talents that inspire in meaning and purpose. Seek meaning in whatever you do. Find a way to combine your abilities and passions with blessing the world. Humility comes as God has orchestrated my amazing calling that has allowed me to travel to distant nations. Looking at every aspect of life as a service to others flows freely with purpose, meaning, and joy. Small miracles happen every day.

Struggles remind us that struggles are not in vain. Beauty is found in broken times. We have "Garden of Gethsemane" moments, when the weight of toils encouraging drinking of the cup. The path to redemption is paved with stones of suffering. Struggle is never weakness. Never question resolve. Disappointment and joylessness are not indicators of failure. Exhaustion is not a sign of defeat.

Transformation on the Street

When any group has joy in its vision, they have strength to meet the problems on the streets. Needs such as food, hygiene, housing, and transportation helps restore dignity, love, and joy.

The goal of a Spirit of Joy Church is to transition people with sound minds, healthy eating, a job, money, skills, and assistance.

A vision quest for joy celebrates healthy families. That quest helps in overcoming addictions, homelessness, recidivism. Restoring needy humans with the confidence of knowing that anything is possible. We are to help them enter into society with dignity.

Amanda Gore, creator of the Joy Project and delightful speaker, is an Australian joy-spotter. Her insights have been shared in conferences, Ted talks, and videos. Her insights include seeing joyous people as feelers of peace, energy filled, enthusiastic, funny, grateful, reverent, optimistic, compassionate, forgiving, and generous with themselves.

While I waited for my food at an outdoor café in Columbia, Missouri, a young waiter was the person of my interest. With a Tiger on his shirt, he moved in and out of the restaurant. He was in such good spirit. His smile and sharing affected other diners. He swirled through the room. He danced virtually as in ballet of dishes and checks. The young man reminded me of myself working in the cafeteria at Carson-Newman College.

I enjoyed overhearing his witty exchanges. A man sitting alone joined in with other diners. We all smiled as the waiter left jauntily to his next chore. That day gave me the full appreciation that joy is contagious.

The young waiter was bursting with life. He brought the joy inside him out into his work. His daily labor of waiting on tables touched people. Smiles became the norm. Joy was this student's driving force.

Life is designed for basic pleasure. A healthy meal, a juicy ripe fruit, a kiss from a loved one. Joy accompanies our wishes and dreams. Joy is not about what we have received, but our conscious choices on behalf of ourselves.

Joy is the outcome of an emotion cycle that begins with a deep longing. Joy is imaging the possibilities. Joy involves the full force of human energy in doing the choices that best use our gifts.

The fall season brings on midlife questions such as: How can I trust God? How can I know God's plans for the me?

When will my troubles end? Focus on getting through the fall times one day at a time. Connect with God every day through quiet and intimate encounters in prayer.

Finding joy is in essence a creative action. It is mystery. It requires courage. Joy sets boundaries between priorities and distractions, detours, and compromises. It is the energy of deep fulfillment and celebration. The fireball flames open as joy gushes more than we will need. We want to share it everywhere.

If a woman finds joy, she needs to actualize her real self. She or he must incarnate that self. To be her true self, more space is needed for creativity. Her world expands. Love is looking for fresh ways of expression. Joy does not stagnate. Her false fabricated self puts together a life that is not open to the present which is becoming the future. Agony and ecstasy intertwine in joy. The real self is sensitive to the cost and pain which brings joy. Perfect joy and perfect affliction have a mysterious unity. Jesus was vulnerable to his affliction. He was aware of the possibility for joy. Jesus' resurrection is like the conventional happy ending to a story. Everyone lives happily ever after. Every soul is interconnected. The mysterious appropriation of joy has repercussions extended to save the world.

Personal perception is a perpetual repetition trying old solutions to solve new problems. The false self concludes that there are no solutions because past attempts failed. The true self refuses to be held down under the crust of continuing habit. Her real self opens up to surprises.

Dancing for the joy of God is found to be at variance with reasonable expectations. "Let this cup pass from me." Jesus thought the idea of passion, death, and resurrection as unreasonable. He understood the joy that was before him. The final note was joy.

Important choices bring perplexities, puzzles as we choose between moderation and abstinence, marriage and singleness, disobedience and cooperation, sanity and insanity, violence and self-control, apathy and action, ignorance and knowledge.

Sharing joy brings empathy. We share from the overflow. We become our best selves. It is essential for our life journeys. Joy is the time for filling up with strength for the next season. If we play monopoly and pass "go" and collect $200. If we miss that square at the start of the game, we will run out of money to buy property later. Personal joy is a life process. It is not the destination, but the fun to share with willingness and enthusiasm. Committing to joy affects those around us. Joy is contagious. Our commitment will result in an overflow of resources and energy to transform the whole world.

Mid-life comes with troubles and challenges. The affirmation, "I will not give up," stirs us on. Other helpful affirmations include: "I am me. I am grateful. I choose joy. This too shall pass. I am not alone. I am powerful. I choose my age. I am enough." Keep telling yourself, you have been given an abundance of everything you need. Counting your blessings with gratitude will multiply blessings. Write what you are thankful for. Your age or season of life does not matter what your talents and gifts are, you have power to make life happen.

Joyful people have an excitement about their dreams. They are in a community where they are cherished and appreciated.

Life is best lived from an eternal perception and perspective. Living eternally is letting God use the circumstances to bring joy. Read Philippians 1:15-18.

On a morning I awoke to a cloudless sunrise. Shakily I crawled out of bed and walked to the dining room. I looked out the window to see a morning alive with color. Jesus said that in his Father's house there are many mansions. As the sun struck blinding rays into my eyes in display of brilliant beauty, I had visions of heaven.

Unbelievable colors, more than any crayon box, will shine in heaven. Every foundation stone will be made with a precious jewel with the glory of God lighting it. More colors will be added to the visible rays of the spectrum. We see only the colors in earthly spectrum visible to the eye.

Understanding the "whys" from God produces another gain that is unbelievable joy. God relaces losses turning them into joy. Life's purposes and callings come into focus as gaining through losing shapes us and others. God's path to glory is also our pathway.

Living from an eternal perspective is to refuse to become sidetracked by petty disagreements with others. I have been published by articles in the *alive now*! magazine to my delight. I love their name . . . alive now. To be alive is to embrace Christ's resurrection power. Being fully alive is catching a passion for the restorative work needed in the world.

Charles Spurgeon said, "You cannot glorify God better than by a calm and joyous life. Let the world know that you serve a good Master."

Joy wins. In walking home with others, we can celebrate small wins. We become the best versions of ourselves. Joy is not a high mountain to climb. Seeing problems, we punish ourselves. Poor performances are quickly condemned. Anxiety, anger, guilt and fear rise to the surface. Success of others is spoken of as luck. Focusing on a mindset, celebrating small wins as achievements. Accept that big wins will not come. Focusing on the end goals, we want to win overnight. Diminished motivation need not keep us from the strength to walk on the top of the mountain. Blindly believing that goals are far away, we give up. A small win might be just around the corner. If we quit, we will never know. Acknowledging small wins sparks reward circuits in the brain. Chemicals are released to give a joyful feeling of pride.

Appreciating small wins and small steps is the difference between failing and succeeding. Lack of gratitude leads down the slippery slope into blindness to small wins.

Homes on Earth: Harbingers of Heavenly Mansions

Inside my earthly home, I cherish my hot cup of tea and the cozy nook in the living room. I dream of unfinished projects. I welcome a home's space. People often say they want to move. Embracing the current home does not mean that we give up on dreams. I am grateful for walking the journey contented and filled with blessings.

We are only here in the world for the blink of an eye. This is not home. That is why the joy that God desires differs from the pleasures on earth. Life is a pilgrimage. Pilgrimages bring clarity. Pilgrimages bond us to others. As we travel, we are not tourists.

I have had incredible spiritual experiences. The power of one friend can change the course. People walk into lives for a reason. Friends teach us. Friends coach us. Friends bring omens from heaven. Friends heal us.

Woven in between the reflections and thoughts stories and ideas in this book are insights and habits that are the foundations of my spiritual life. Give joy a chance. Nobody walks their journey alone. We need companions. God wants us to live an excellent life. Questing for excellence gives us sheer joys. Excellence learns.

Mediocrity repeats mistakes. Mediocrity hates ordinary, everyday acts. It distracts. Excellence calls us to transform life into a prayer. To be transformed is to be converted. Conversion does not end with a one-time experience. Conversion is an on-going journey. Grace invites us to collaborate with God in the daily conversion.

Every moment of every day, every situation, every person we encounter is another opportunity for joy. We do not stand still in conversion. No break is allowed. The continuous effort to receive everything God is pouring into you as you walk others home to be with God.

Placing God at the center makes sense of life. The purpose of existence is wrapped up in God. Separation from God loses meaning.

Enjoy the moment and the place where you live. Joy is contagious. Put everything down and relish this moment. Even if you realize that the current home is not the eternal home. Counter negatives with what you love. Images of beautiful homes and tours of new homes bring a kind of discontentment. Find joy in writing in a journal what you like about your current home. Create memories with loved ones. Enjoy your children in each growing season. We can't stop time. Enjoy life now.

When you and the family look back, they will be happy to see you in the photos. Discover what gives joy. Taking a walk together, baking, or playing makes us smile.

Hug and kiss your spouse in front of the children. One day they will remember your marriage when they are in their own marriage. Hold hands. Hug. Kiss. Talk. Plan.

Enjoy the million little things that matter. Think in eternal terms. Spend time with those that matter. Everything else can wait.

Inside each soul is a pilot light. In my kitchen, I use a gas stove. By turning a switch, I ignite a flame of fire, or I put it out. People have an inner flame that can be blown out with one breath. Making another person's day or extinguishing their spirit causes joyless people to blow out the pilot light I the way we blow out a candle. I pray that my writing this book will ignite joy and never be blown it out.

Our mission is to ignite the spirits of those we encounter. Listless eyes and shriveled spirits never dance, twinkle or sparkle.

Successful habits equal success. Adapting to new routines is not easy. Addiction to joy will lead us to the next steps. Understand the importance of the present moment. Reward yourself for each small win.

Investing in the "little million things" for a long time will result in doing big wins. Achieving small wins gives motivation to expect more. Break goals into smaller ones. Create small achievable goals to see progress more clearly. Smaller goals shield from procrastination. Reward yourself. Flexible time limits increase joy capacity. Track progress in a journal. Seeing small wins in writing is reward itself.

Obsessing on end goals makes joy impossible. Try thinking of walking up a huge mountain. Descending will bring a pleasant stop off and relaxation on the way home. Marking off milestones yields rewards to celebrate.

Zeal, enthusiasm, and zest are part of the "jouissance," a French expression. Joy is that something that puts a twinkle in the eye, lights up the face, sets a spring in our step. Joy is like the sun radiating, shining, and permeating everything around your circle. Nobody can muster an appreciation of joy. When life appears dull and routine and empty, we do not expect anything to go right.

It is the joy inside us that counts. Joy and contentment come from within. It is the overflow from our choices. We draw in what we think. Change the thinking, decide the beginning now. Make the rest of your life be what you want. Never discredit or put yourself down. Banish the fear of failure. God has more joy moments ahead for each one. Joy is available to the least of these. An incurable invalid who accepts the pain of her constriction shares in the cross. That weak person does more to establish justice than a multitude of reformers. She prays for other people. And each is empowered for great things.

Each child of God is a prodigal son. God reminds us of the joy of his father's home. Walking each other home in practical ways places us on the road towards it.

In a quaint little bookstore in Norwich, England, I bought a book by Peter Brice on his fight for joy during his depressed periods. It has gone out of print.

His bibliography listed some books that helped Brice to discover joy. Some contained special sections which suit the poor concentration common with mental health issues.

He also listed passages from the Bible. He appears to be a scholar, and he has dealt with scripture. His method was effective. He breathed deeply to relax his body. He read the Bible slowly several times, he would close his eyes and ponder. He would jot down any phrase that caught his spirit, and thoughts that were stimulated.

Genesis 32:23-32, II Samuel 1:19-27, Psalms 23, 91, and 121, Psalm 51, 88, and 103, 139:11-12, Ecclesiastes 3:1-8, Isaiah 43:18-20 and 55, Matthew 4:1-11, 5:3-12, 6:25-34, 23:13-33, Mark 5:1-20, Luke 7:36-50, 15:11-31, John 7:53-8:11, Romans 8:31-39, I Corinthians 13-14:1, Galatians 5:22-23, James 3:17, I John 4:7-21 were the passages he read.(Peter Brice, *On the Edge: Wrestling with God in Depression*, pp. 255-256.)

Prayer for the Joy of Companionship

God, I am so grateful for the joy of companionship. Thank you for placing family and friends and Christian companions in each life. What a joy to meet and to have fellowship with our brothers and sisters.

God most holy, as days slow down and crimson sunset catches suntanned hills and golden valley in the last glow of fall, quiet me with joy. As I walk with others let me not be too busy, insensitive, or unaware to open my eyes, my ears, and my intuition that I sense Your mercy and love.

Thanks for our wonderful friend in Jesus. He is our never-failing companion. We are grateful for Jesus' promise that he will never forsake us or leave us alone. In every season of life, Jesus will never fail us, even during times that we are forgetful and foolish. In Christ, we have received newness and became new creatures in Christ. What joy we have in our friend Jesus to give the gift of companionship throughout earthly life. Lord, we realize that there is no unending bliss on earth. Thank you for always being present, always loving us, always ready to add a dimension of joy in everything we do. In Jesus' name. Amen.

Practical Application

Get your Bible and read the verses that Brice used and see how it helps.

Add to your list of what you are thankful for in this season.

Write in your journal your reaction to the thought that joy is not a place to which you have traveled to on your journey, but your manner of traveling.

Reflect on the following thought by C.S. Lewis, "No soul that seriously and consistently seeks joy will ever miss it. Those who seek find. Those who knock, the door will be opened."

What necessary people in your life do you appreciate? Make a least of eight or ten. After their name, mention reasons why. Take a moment to pray for them.

WINTER

"The deepest part of the human soul longs For the joy that God has prepared for us."

--Roma Downey

Winter

Winter is the quietest of seasons. It is a time of joy, love, believing, dlaughter, and snow. I hear more laughter on the street at Advent time in December. There is a joyful spirit in the air. We endure the smell of cold and snow.

Yes, snow. That white stuff is frozen rain. Snow sweeps the blues away. The man, Norman Vincent Peale, who anointed me as the minister of joy to the world, said, "Christmas waves a magic wand over the world and behold everything is softer and more beautiful."

That magic of winter brings togetherness. People are cheerful and joyful. As faithful carolers sing near our home, we offer hot chocolate, coffee or tea to bring joy with each sip. They might delight with the water boiling on the stove to make hot tea. They listen as the oven bleeps as cookies finish baking.

Bright sunshine marches across long frozen fields. Red-orange robins fight blue jays for plump berries. Snow envelops. Frost inhibits. Winter shoves us indoors. Braving cold winters reveals the quiet ways of God slip up on us. We are not overly concerned about the scheme of things. Living in the right place at the right time is not diminished. Faith undergirds us. Loved ones assure us. At the end of the road, promises of heaven await as we walk together. Grab a spiritual road map. Understand each season.

Singing reminds us of the love of Jesus. Jesus desires an intimate connection as branches to a vine. Pick up your cup. It symbolizes a cup of joy. Holding your cup, imagine connecting to God in Jesus. Imagine his filling your cup causing his joy to be ours. Fill it to the brim.

Joy is not based on outer circumstances. It perceives inner commitment to keep joy in every season.

During the winter passage, Gail Sheehy shares some questions: What new ventures or adventures can you now dare to try? What old shells can you slough off? How can you best give back? What investments in learning and changes in lifestyle are you willing to undertake to make all the extra years ahead livable? How long do you want to live? (Gail Sheehy, *New Passages: Mapping Your Life Across Time*, p. 701)

Use these questions to ponder the winter season of life. Answer them in a journal. Take clues from nature. Rest like animals do. Winter recharges. Spiritual ideas abound. Restlessness is typical. Be strategic about spring plans. Rest in the grace of God.

Wintertime. A chill up our spines comes as winter whistles through our cold lips. Winter means frigid discomfort and discontent. Icy shadows skate across frozen ponds. Short days, long nights. Gray clouds and harsh winds sting our faces. We walk each other with grim determination. Walking with heavy garb, we trudge on.

Warming up alongside a crackling fire, listening to music, we look in joyful anticipation for Christmas and New Year's Eve. Listening in quiet reverence is special. Take a long walk over the freshly fallen white flakes. When winter ends, look up as a wiser, stronger, deeper soul.

Embracing the Joys of Winter

Embracing this winter season is cozy cocooning indoors. Committing to spending time outdoors makes colder days much bearable by boosting both our physical, spiritual, and mental wellness. Healthy people have a positive wintertime mindset. They believe winter is packed with opportunities for enjoyment and fulfillment. This positive mindset leads to overall wellness. During bitter winters, the warmth and glow of a fireplace sings of comfort and hope in the darkness. Winter is a quieting time to rest in the warmth of our soul's hearth. The indwelling fire is reignited so we can live with joyful enthusiasm.

This fire opens our souls, removes fear, instills hope and healing. Joy leads to wisdom, because joy connects us to all that we are. It stimulates the immune system, increases energy, and gives us clarity.

Many mountain resorts offer discounts or free skiing for older adults. Some resorts offer grays on trays an opportunity for snowboarding. Winter is the favorite season with ski buffs. Snow lovers resent those who don't enjoy cold and snow.

Age Gracefully

The winter season requires toughness. Fear comes in winter. We do not desire a wrinkly face or a stooped body. We become paranoid about slipping and falling in the shower. Energy feels heavy. Feeling weak in body, mind, and spirit, the false self, we act sluggish. Out of flow, we disconnect. Negative scripts creep in. Life becomes a heavy weight. Lacking focus brings on despair, not inspiration. Knocking out of flow comes with certain moments, energy in the air. These things show a need of alignment with the true self.

It happens. I know.

Culture bombards us with thoughts that aging is to be dreaded. Independence slipping away is horrid. Pretending change is not happening will not stall the season. Aging is inescapable. God planned it. Greater joy has been designed. Awaiting older people are new gifts reserved for late life. Bodies are uniquely made. Put love in motion by using all senses and imagination. Change and loss are constants. Journeys of discovery come after multiple losses. Take time suggesting companions to walk with you.

God calls us to joy in every season. Saint Francis took Paul's injunction "to rejoice in the Lord always" quite literally. His joy led Francis to lift his feet. His arms were extended toward the sky. He jumped around in joy. Not afraid to let the joy inside the body, he acted in the play of joy.

Fixing eyes on growing old, the elderly think in negative images. Treasures are right before us. Focus on God. Discover abiding joy that comes with a long life.

This book should get into the hands of everybody. What a lovely gift to encourage those in later seasons of life to feel less lonely. Walking together with each other, joy happens. All caregivers including nurses, physicians, and ministers will emphasize with challenges beloved ones face.

When we are young, we are busy chasing our dreams, embroiled in our plans and making a living out of what we know and are enabled to do. We enjoy the closeness and togetherness of family. In our seasons of youth, age is no perceived bar. The fear of death is a non-issue. We think there are no limits, and even if there are, we don't accept any.

In the winter season, old age causes us to experience the periphery of our vision, the occasional creaking sound in our bones, pain in the back, issues with blood pressure, sugar levels, memory, and weak knees.

We often check our savings and investments to ensure that we have enough to see us through our wintering age. The reality of a waning body unsettles a calm mind. These winter difficulties are inevitable. Being positive with eternal views, aging people know grace, wisdom, and stability. Carrying joy in the heart heals the winter moments. A joyful life, lived in peaceful bliss, is the best existence to know. In all seasons of life, we can hold on to positive vibrations and newfound energy that encourages us to look to the future with high hopes, eternal hopes.

The connection of the soul is more important than being dazzled by external beauty. Maturity lets us slow down and enjoy the process. When desires stop pushing us in every direction, we experience inexplicable peace. Joy is a piercing desire, a mystical longing, homesickness for a home we scarcely remember.

Matthew Fox shares immense insight in his 532-page book, *Sheer Joy*. His writing is styled in a sitting where he is in conversation with Thomas Aquinas on aspects of joy. Fox's book is a conduit for spiritual psychology. The author gives an exploration of spirituality implicit in all of Aquinas's work and is a hermeneutic applied to his thoughts. By interviewing or having an imaginary conversation, the book makes Aquinas accessible. Fox wrote, "The experiences of God should not be restricted to the few or to the old." The book is long, but seekers of joy will keep reading just as children read Harry Potter. (Matthew Fox, *Sheer Joy: Conversations with Thomas Aquinas*, pp. 1-532)

Joy is our destiny. To know who we are, we need joy. This upwelling of the soul is an experience of the love of God. As we fall asleep at night and awaken in morning, we know that all is well.

My introduction to Julian of Norwich came during my study at Oxford. The study made more sense as students visited the cell of Julian as background. She lived from 1341 until 1415. This beloved saint was a mystic, a healer, an author, a counselor. She is now widely revered, but not while she was alive. I felt her faith as we made the pilgrimage to Julian's cell. The cell was attached to an old church. She received 16 gruesome showings. These magic showings revealed to her something extraordinary. "All is well. Joy is the pure delight in being alive for we are living joy," was her thesis.

About 20 graduate psychology students talked about Julian, her times, her thoughts, her poverty, her plagues, and the brutality in this beautiful medieval town called Norwich. As we sat in her small cell, we felt the presence and spirit of this woman who dedicated herself to her calling of sharing a message that was greater than the bloody brutality of the times.

I shared my insight at Saint Benedict Conference Center in Nebraska. I have found more inspiration in the practical spirituality of Julian of Norwich as I felt in my soul, "All is well." Imagine the gift she gave the world God's joy to fill us. As Julian wrote, "The fulness of joy is to behold God in all things."

Julian uncovered the deeper levels of joy until that joy that streams from God is realized in each breath. Every increase in joy is an increase in strength and peace. Joy is a divine dance. The music in the soul is joy.

Thomas Merton taught, "The silence of the spheres is the music of a wedding feast. The more we persist in misunderstanding the phenomena Of life, the more we analyze them into strange finalities and complex purposes of our own, the more we involve ourselves in absurdity and sadness. But it does not matter much, because no despair can change reality, or stain the joy of the cosmic dance which is always there."

Wear Your Winter Season with Pride

Souls never lesson with age. Each year we bring more for the journey. Each year we become who we are. Younger is not always better. When winter brings surgery, we'd rather have a surgeon with a few wrinkles above a freshly minted physician with a spring in her step. When we searched for a builder to construct our customed built home, we wanted that builder to have built but one or two new homes. Wintertime brings us experience in spades. We must stop apologizing for our age. Wear it proudly. We do miss the color pigment in our hair. And most men miss even having hair. We miss smooth skin, the illusion that we are indestructible, and the energy to make love all night. Retirees have more time, money, and experience which means opportunities to pursue interests, to travel, to reinvent ourselves.

We can continue to do mental transformation and ask questions we had during the spring and summer seasons such as "Who do I want to be? What is important to me? To what will we pay honor as we transition to glorious eternal life in heaven? What are the priorities?"

When we take everything for granted, we need to step into a climate of joy. Be aware about wonders of life. So much in life captures joy. If the sun shines, enjoy the warm rays. If it rains, enjoy the fresh air. If the weather is cold, we dress warm and drink a glass of tea.

Life is short. Each moment is perfect and precious. Living fully in the present moment, we sense we are living to the fullest. We celebrate.

Intense joy is felt as we celebrate the miracle of love. Every life is a full life. We cannot how long we will live. We do not know the day of our death. Live each day as fully as possible. A key plan is to live each day as if it was the first day or the last day.

The strategy in love is to love more. Death brings awareness of the importance of those we love. That is a sustaining force. When someone close dies, joy will burn through our grief. We will eternally be thankful for each other and for life.

Power outages in winter bring gratitude for the power that keeps home running on all cylinders. Warmth, light, food, and technology comes from power that we do not see or think about.

Seeing God's influence on and in the journey is essential for joy. As soon as my grandson as a baby could do things, he became joyful. After he was born, my daughter brought him to see me. I was thrilled. I held his infant body for hours praying over him. He really grew a bit that day. And he smiled.

Babies explore and accomplish new movements and the joy shows in their faces. Joy flows into parents and grandparents. And we smile.

Opening eyes to experience joy in babies being born, seasons bringing changes, and the body working miraculously each day. Recall some event that felt terrible at the time. God turned it into the best thing that ever happened. Remember times when you felt guidance from God. Ask God to come so clearly into your life that you just know it was from a divine source.

John Killinger writes on Luke 2:1-20, "Luke reveals in a major theme of his gospel that is associated with Jesus and the kingdom of God. Characteristically for Luke, the shepherds having learned the joyful news, in turn become its bearers. They went back to the hills, "glorifying and praising God for all they had heard and seen. The joy of the kingdom is that contagious." (John Killinger, *The Gospel of Contagious Joy*, pp. 21-23)

When you are walking beside another, you soak in the courage knowing joy is always available. No matter how bad the situation is, we can seek God's help. Sunshine returns with bursts of joy.

If we can become the change, family and friends will notice. The knowledge of being loved, even when you are separated from each, will sustain us with inner strength and comfort.

Any relationship can be complete without ending. Completion is not a finality. If we were to die tomorrow, we have no regrets. Nothing is really undone. Eternal joy renews the circle of significant relationships. Life-affirming live will still be as in the beginning. Even in mourning, those so loved merge into our psyche and soul. They continue to influence thoughts and emotions.

Doctors of the soul give healing with interpretation, analysis, listening and therapy. There is limited space for those confined. Incarceration or hospitalization is routine. Intercede for those whose needs are too painful to bear. Comfort those who go to bed with less faith felt. Circumstances unsteady them. Disease will not be healed.

Injuries cannot be reversed. Relationships are permanently ruptured. Death is inevitable.

This book and my sharing have created a biography of joy. Biographies of joy help us to look at life in a constructive, positive way. Joy is what lets us let down our guard. When filled with joy, we feel self-confident and accept all that there is.

Begin your autobiography in the spring season thinking of childhood. Curiosity, unlimited smiles, singing, and snuggling as your parents read you a book. In the summer season, birthdays, Christmas mornings, or an exciting family trip are joyfully celebrated. In the fall teen years joy came during a piano recital, swimming, drawing, Joy begins in closeness with parents. Remember the first time you fell in love.

Winter joys are visiting family, reading books, watching movies, holding new babies, and taking your vitamins, especially vitamin "J."

Moments are precious. Be thankful for the gifts of the moments. Moments and joy are fused. Gratitude expands souls. It is an act of generosity. Joyfully we share what we have, not what we lack.

The world that our children and grandchildren will live in a rapidly changing one. Their future world is impossible to anticipate. It will be different from anything we have known. I want to assure the future generations of my unconditional love. I have attempted to wish them well.

Thank God for all you have. You will become much stronger when problems come in your path. When we enjoy life more, emotional frequency increases. Thoughts generate emotion. Emotion generates frequency.

Discard the dead weight and eliminate it. Incredible energy will build in your soul. We do not have to feel wistful about our past seasons.

The bright potential that comes in winter commands all of our attention.

A Winter Walk in Nebraska

During the winter of 2021, Nebraskans were greeted by a magical wonderland outside our windows. I sat at the table drinking green tea, watching thick snow blanket the street in front of our home.

Suddenly we got warmly dressed. Neighborhood men with snow blowers were hurrying. Elmwood is a wonderful place to live. In winter, no matter how hard the snow is blowing, our sidewalks and streets are plowed. Old men find excitement to get out their snow blowers to help the community. As soon as snowflakes begin to fall, every driveway Would have an old man, or a young one who mowed lawns in the summertime. I smile at the comfortable predictability. These folks find joy in the doing.

Some nearby farmers bring tractors into town to blow driveways in less than two minutes for each home. We have never had to plow the sidewalk or the driveway.

Living in a small town is vital to my joy and well-being. Joy cannot and should never be ignored. Joy makes life worth living. We cannot understand human beings unless we understand joy and how it comes to be. With joy, our souls are open, giving our living fluidity and contentment. Dr. Chris Meadows, professor in the doctoral program at Vanderbilt University Divinity School, said in a seminar on joy, "Joy is central to the spiritual life, part of the fabric of a spiritual reality that transcends religious traditions. Joy is the capacity that is enhanced by faith in that joy is intrinsic to what it means to be human."

Meadows at Vanderbilt and also scholars at Yale University's Faith and Culture Center, have intimated that joy is a concept independent of happiness.

Joy in the Seasons of Life

If joy is merely a symbol for happiness, efforts to create a science of Joy would be redundant with the science of happiness. I have spent a lifetime in pursuit of a systematic investigation of joy.

Most definitions of joy are too vague. Recent work through a grant from the Templeton Foundation for Yale Divinity School has resulted in advances in conceptualizing joy and how it differs from happiness. Differing from mood states, joy is an emotional state with news of something good or positive in life circumstances.

Joy is scientifically interesting not because it is a positive emotion, but because of its distinctive character. Joy must be experienced. Joy is difficult to define, but through all seasons, people contend that we know it when we experience it, and we know it when we lose it.

Joy is different from happiness. Happiness is how good we feel over all seasons. Joy comes in a moment of time. I agree that joy is an intense, momentary experience of positive emotion. These moments are brief but contribute to overall happiness.

Joy deepens our relationships with God. Joy connects us with people we care about. Celebrating a beloved's joy increase the intimacy and closeness that we enjoy in a relationship.

Joy sharpens our minds. Research shows that we make better choices when we are joyful. Joy helps us form new habits. When we build joy into our habits, we are more likely to stick with them and to create lasting shifts in our souls. Moments of joy helps our bodies to recover from stress and disappointment and rejection.

Walking is good for the soul. Walking is a spiritual practice that helps in finding the way to God. Joy and wellness result. Connecting and listening strengthen relationships, fulfill dreams, and move your insides with transformation. Joyless folks look everywhere outside themselves to satisfy needs. Joy boosters act in love bringing positive change.

Clean out the clutter. Sweep the corners in your soul. Make room for God. Committing to spiritual practice to increase joy is a good goal. Joy causes spiritual practices. Focus on the ends not the means. Walking each other home is critical. Deep inside we know we are beloved of God. Seasons pass. Culture, trauma, and experience causes a disconnection. Sharing life's journey is critical. The world is desperate to realize that each is beloved.

Love is who we are.

Imagine yourself without a thing. No family, no friends, no possessions. All school friends have vanished. You are banned from Facebook and all social media. Your job has flown out the window. Your home has evaporated into thin air. Who are we now?

God's love does not come with prayers answered, blessings bestowed, promises intended in love. God sees us as precious. We are of immense value even if we have lost everything just as Job did.

Life and love with joy comes for parents and grandparents when receiving art by children. Today I received a lovely ceramic of my grandson Ethan's art as he composed the morning bulletin for Bradley Hills Presbyterian Church in Bethesda. Every morning I drink from a cup of tea with Ethan's drawing as a small child printed on the cup.

Notice how the joy of a parent or grandparent imparts priceless value to a picture drawn by a small child. The. Love of God pours immeasurable worth to everything we do. God misses nothing. Expressing my pride I have every note, letter, and photo of Ethan's life. His mom, my daughter Linda, has placed his work on her refrigerator.

During a children's sermon at First Christian Church in Weeping Water, Nebraska, I told the children that when they did a loving deed, God posts each one's deed on God's refrigerator in heaven.

Seeing our life's artwork on God's fridge is the ultimate goal. God is love. God is life. God is joy. God fills emptiness. Going from one end of the known universe to the other at the speed of light would take 30 billion years. God has a huge refrigerator.

Transforming into the real authentic self will change the soul into a tenderly affectionate being. Where there was once a stone, now there is reality. God builds us, renews us, invigorates us as you see the world through clear glasses.

Look into a mirror. See the real you. Love that authentic self. The Father knows himself. The knowledge of God is perfect. Eternal. God created everything. God created us. Life on earth is transitional. Placing us in time, we are prepared for eternity. Read I John 3:2.

Without love, there is no strength. We stare at life with terrified eyes. That's the reason I work to free those who are emotionally crippled. They are loveable. Self-concepts are wrapped in God. God tells us we have worth and beauty and intrinsic value. The opinions of the Creator count. Without love, we are debilitated and sapped of happiness. Adolescents enervates with feelings of instability and unsubstantiality. People in all seasons of life live insipid lives, running in every direction but into the hands of God. God wants to send a love day, a valentine. That proves that we are the property of Jesus. God knows us and loves us.

Our possibilities are unlimited as we realize how we are beautiful, unique, and usable.

Valentine's day comes in winter. We have been incarnated for love. As living beings, our essence is love. Our bodies house our love and joy vibrations. Be more aware with this vibration by speaking more compassionately to those we are given to love. Live more mindfully to help incorporate the joy that lives within us. Living for God brings extreme love as vast as the universe. God loves us more than our best friend. God loves each of us more than any human being could love us.

No walls separate us. No bodyguards shield us from God's attention. No appointment is needed. Nobody waits in line. God lives inside us.

Using this energetic frequency will produce experiences that benefit you in the winter seasons. Remember we are energetic beings of joy who are interconnected. I have every Valentine card that was ever given to me. There is no one that is not capable of being loved. It was my joy in grade school to give Valentines to everyone, especially those who needed love more than others. Heaven rejoices as we love ourselves as God loves us. Seeing ourselves as beloved grants the capacity to bless the Lord. You have a place in God's heart. God showers us with blessings. These are valentines of sweet, pure intimacy. Our human valentines are not the same as the divine ones. Human expressions of love appear inept next to the spiritual. The human spirit is capable of doing nice kind things. The human spirit can be brave, noble, joyful, and good.

A regenerated soul has God living inside. Read Galatians 5:16. Everything we have and that we are is through, because of, God now on earth, and in eternity. The gifts of the Spirit are ours because we are free to be used by God. We take the gifts willingly and openly because we love the Lord. Nothing can conquer us, not even death. All that we touch is turned into love.

Love means loving faults, warts, and ugliness. Love comes not despite but because lovers love unconditionally. Deep love is rare. The love of God is pure. God knows and guides us, seeing potential God is loving and patient.

The person who gives us love valentines is a gift. Given the opportunity to experience love teaches us that we are worth loving. Love God first and love will be inside of you. Put on the glasses of

God. If we could see others as God does, we would be valentines to the world.

Loving yourself is a way of loving God. We are made in the image of God. We are a part of the Divine. If we treat ourselves badly, we treat God badly.

Feel love inside. Be connected to God and you will be treated very good. Allow God to be close and intimate. Treat every person as if they wear a sign that says, "God lives here."

Without our conscious awareness, God prepares us for showdown decisions. During a conference with more than a thousand in attendance, I felt God speaking during my quiet prayer time. I asked God to send revival at the meeting. I asked God to allow me to be an instrument to revive joy. "Make me not a great organ, but one of the empty pipes through which spiritual power will bring a movement for salvation.

In unbroken, intimate communion, I offered not actions, but the whole soul, mind, body, and self to God. I felt my words of commitment calling me to hold the world in my hands as God does. God opened doors, and fantastic opportunities began to happen.

I conceived the conception of gaining through losing all rights to myself. My grandson Ethan sent me a framed picture with the words, "Find joy in the journey."

Live with Your Authentic Self

Joy comes from a place of honoring and living with our authentic selves. Courage helps us become who we are. Tough challenges will come. Stand your ground and in winter, you will come to the other side feeling less burdened. You will enjoy life with less struggle.

We think that when stressors are gone or medication is reduced, we can go on at the same pace. Even small events make demands on emotional energy. We might journal to record the demands, so we are aware of needing rest and relaxation. There is real difficulty to live within ourselves. We learn to listen to the cycles of exhaustion and energy.

Authentic people evoke images that threaten our fabricated joy. The self wants joy, but it continues joy-repudiating withdrawal. Marathon runners prepare themselves with years of steady training. Only then do they dare take a place at the starting line. When it comes to imitating the love of God, we must learn to walk before we run. Sprinting down the track before toning muscles is foolish. Inevitably, this leads to spiritual cramps.

Beginners who walk with others need spiritual preparation. Joy is a possibility for each of us. Joy is a mighty centrifugal force that wears away the hard rind of a soul solicitude for the authentic self, others, and God.

Living in the presence of God is a dance for joy. The presence of the Spirit is powerful. Jesus does not leave us to our own devices to know his joy. Jesus' presence demands response. His presence brought calm. Jesus ignited every human emotion. Imagine walking down dusty roads with him. Imagine hearing his parables. Imagine Jesus coming to your home for lunch.

Closing the gap between life without his presence and life that Jesus invites to experience, the more sheer joy we will know. Joy is lasting and complete.

Without joy, we are left alone in wanting something that's missing. Jesus came to immerse us in joy. Walking each other home is the only path to joy. The goal of the spiritual journey is complete joy. Grace and awareness enable us to want what God wants. The joy we seek requires applying the teachings of Jesus. Life is short. Do it now. Joy is found in the present moment. Live each moment passionately with God. Live the best possible life. Forget yesterday. Forget all yesterdays. Past is gone. The gospel works. Connected to living the gospel is the amount of joy for the journey.

This book plumbs deeply the joy that little by little steps gets us ever closer. My prayer is that this life-long exploration can serve to aid in recognition and embracing the joy. Joy is powerful enough to slice through the self we now live with reality. This truth remains eternal in any culture or season. Some have created an alienated self. The opposite is the authentic self. Alienated selves live in bondage. The term alienated self carries a negative connotation. This state of suffocating engagement causes isolated and helpless frustration. Alienation shuts us off from liberating possibilities by hostile external circumstances.

Liberating authentic selves break the chains. They crack the shell to find what joy strength to reveal the horribly corruption of that isolated self and the shimmering promise of its destiny. Divine Presence is creative, eliciting reality, intimacy and meaning. God is available. God evokes inside us a grateful and joyful longing to be conduits of what we can experience.

There is no promise that if we are a presence for each other, fellow humans, or God. We must be presence for ourselves. Woven into the fabric of our existence is this enduring reality. This is hard to accomplish. We will be tempted to bypass the true self by focusing on sham substitute. That sham self is like a weathercock, blown in worldly directions for a lifetime.

Self-images shift with the passage of each season. Our values, interests, our perceptions of the world and other people, fears, ambitions, motivations, and inhibitions are not predictable. The self is sensitive to changes in the atmosphere.

When a person takes her center of gravity to be her "me," it is easy to spot it as egoism. She has an inflated ego to esteem her attractiveness, talents, strengths with an infuriating cockiness. The reality is that she thinks too little of herself. Her self-assurance is a sham. She holds nagging anxiety. She tirelessly checks and rechecks her conflictions. Far from arrogant confidence, she is tormented with a crushing sense of impotence and doom. She fixates on her own needs and that is debilitating.

Once we accept God's invitation to open ourselves enables us to find deep and authentic joy. We live as authentic human beings if we dwell on the clearing of the true self after we have discovered it. Brokenness changes to wholeness. We become dwellers, at home in and with ourselves. We are no longer at home with frustrated strangers in a strange land. Unbreakably connected to God, we know we are worthy as we resemble Joy, seeing ourselves as we really are.

Joy is experienced by the person to and for whom we make our true available, creative, and intimate all that emanates from the presence of God. The spiritual state of being with humanity is in intimate relationships rather than co-existing alongside as fragmentation has been given to wholeness. The kingdom of heaven is the blessed place that we become fully human. We belong to the same body of Christ filled with love and joy. In recognizing her true Christ-self, she has ways to be

To become unemployed or to be with no official standing is a stigma. To be a pensioner on retirement is to be derived of status. To be a poor person with little money is to be of no account. God assures us that we are loved for who we are and not for what we can do. We behave as if our value depends on what we achieve in our work. We are tempted to say yes when we know we must say no. We become anxious when we do not reach the highest standards. The ingrained sense of responsibility catches us unawares. To know who we are we must be aware of limits and limitations. We have to say no at the beginning than to have to confess later that we do not have the time or the stress of over-commitment.

As we complete journeys, assume the best of us all until we are proven wrong. If something is worth doing, we do not have to be inhibited by fears of failure. Joyful people do not get upset by criticism. It says nothing about our worthiness. Anger and unhappiness come with unrealistic expectations of ourselves and others. Falls and upsets are par for our life course. These do not signify failure. These times give us a chance to learn from our mistakes and to recognize the progress made toward a healthy spirit. We have wounds to carry, and we are not in the same season. We are in the process of being our authentic selves.

We cannot give other people our advice. We have to find our own solutions. As we continue to exist in our pain, we know we cannot escape. Running away just brings more pain later. The only way forward is through the pain. As you keep walking in the path, you will meet joy. Invite others to walk with you. Our eyes become Jesus' eyes. Our hands are Christ's hands. Be close to those who are loved. Hug your parents and grandparents. Find joy in the birth of a child. Delight in music and art. See God in a mountain vista. Respect and love others. Experience God's presence. Accept the joy that comes from the palm of God's loving hand.

Will there be sex in heaven? Sex is a wonderful gift from God. God delights in every passionate feeling that accompanies exgod created it. Bodies know soaring pleasure and excitement. Depths of intimacy in sex has nothing equal. Sex is physically enthralling. Couples united together in those moments desire to be with nobody else. Holy, godly, wonderful sex is beyond description.

God created us to be completely satisfied. The life we live in faith is a delight. Taste buds enjoy food. Faith means to enjoy God. Nothing compares. Jesus is now in heaven. Nothing is better. Speculating about heaven humbles us. Communion with God is for eternity.

Climb a mountain range. Hike towards its peak. Expect a marvelous scene at the top. Coming to the summit, a dozen more peaks are viewed in the distance. Mysteries of God are never exhausted. Only God is never tired from loving finite creatures.

Sexuality is a precious gift. In heaven, I believe we will enjoy everything that sex points toward. Both the delight and unsatisfied longings that come with sex points us toward heaven.

Walking Each Other Home

Eternity dwarfs our earthly life span, yet it dignifies our journey with the undeniable suggestion of continued existence. Eternity is a quality of life. Expecting joy is not a fanciful pipe dream. God intended humans to live forever. We want to know what an eternal heaven will be like. We desire to know more. We are like children anticipating a really fun summer vacation. During an 80-year lifetime, we do recreation and watch television for about 15 years.

Next year, God willing, I shall become 80 years old. The average person that age will have spent six years riding in an automobile. Three years reading. Six years in school. Seven years eating. Fifteen years working. Nearly 30 years sleeping. Worshiping for a year, unless you are a preacher. Following the earthly journey, there is joy in union with God.

We cannot figure out the particulars. Heaven is not like the earth. Natural senses can't perceive it. Read I Corinthians 2:9. Heaven is better than we can imagine. The best and most beautiful earthly scenes are a shadow of the reality of heaven. Nothing feels better than going home. For a long lifetime I spent much of my time away from home. There is such joy in coming home to your own space. This joy is feeling at home with our true selves, with who we are and what we are doing. Familiar surroundings, comfortable and warm, and seeing friends expends the joy.

Home is taken for granted. Jesus had no home. Read Luke 9:58. Jesus came into the world as a tiny ovum in an unmarried woman's womb. The manger had no reservation. He was born in a stable. He never went home. Visiting the region where he was from, he never traveled home. Jesus had no earthy home.

Being away from home was the most difficult part of my travels. I missed the feel of my bed, firm pillows, food in the refrigerator, and things. Ministry on the road includes feelings associated with being unsettled, unmoored, and disoriented. I yearn for home. Mostly I look for my heavenly home. Arriving home is a foreshadow of the final journey home to be with God in an eternal home.

Growing up in East Tennessee, I never imagined that I would live anywhere else. Now I feel home is in Nebraska, but I yearn for heaven.

God loves us. God does not shorten our lives in order to get us back. When our days are done, the creator welcomes us home. This life is a gift. We misunderstand what is behind it. Going home, we gain eternal life. Woven more tightly than we could imagine in our dim glimpses of the mysteries and delights.

When our family constructs a jigsaw puzzle, we don't have a clear picture. We start with the edges. We search for the corners. As more and more pieces are fitted into place, each piece gets easier and quicker. We will never construct a complete picture of our eternal home before we get there.

We are finite. Earthly ears can't hear many pitches on the sound spectrum. Bodies can't feel physical sensations without healthy nerve endings. One-third of life is in the physical state of sleep. We have little consciousness of the world around us.

Without calories and sleep, fatigue is unavoidable. The body gets restless during long stretches of time. Aches and stomach pangs keep us distracted. As years pass, the body tires easily as it grows leathery, stiff, and frail.

Physical life eventually breaks. Vigorous exercise, the best nutrition, nothing can stop us wearing down. Read Ecclesiastes 12:5-7. The point of God making heaven and earth could not be to have it all end, and for humans to simply cease to exist.

Heaven will be filled with joy and continuous celebration. Guilt, anger, anxiety, and fear will not be needed in a place filled with only joy.

Completing all the puzzle with all the pieces enables us to finish the puzzle that reveals the perfect home where we will live forever. Heaven will not fade away. We shall feel constant excitement and anticipation. Even the Bible gives only sketches and brief glimpses. We will be wowed as God personally shows us the delights of our heavenly home.

Imagine never needing to say good-bye to anyone. Think of what we will be capable of in glorified bodies. Consider endless opportunities to meet and talk with fellow believers. Not only will we renew life with as many as third generations of unknown ancestors. Perhaps I shall meet my 28th great grandfather Robert the Bruce.

My grandfather died before I was born. Seeing him will clear the picture. The sheer joy and treasure of every day on earth could not be contained in each instant of eternity in heaven. A thousand earth years add up to little more than one day of eternity.

Our reborn spirit already exists in us in the same way that it will exist after the body dies. We will be refined like gold from base ore. Conscious existence will be extended. It is not exterminated. Read I Corinthians 15: 51-53. We regain our personality when we arrive in heaven. Eternity makes age a moot point. Heavenly bodies are ageless.

Seeing stars in day light is impossible. With the human eye, we view pinpricks of light. We have no idea about the magnitude of these stars as suns. The Master Teacher will teach us more than we can imagine. Read First Corinthians 13:9-12.

We shall see clearly in our jigsaw puzzle with revelations from God. Jesus grew in wisdom and stature before his Parent and humankind. Read II Corinthians 4:18-5:1.

We are one family divided into more than 200 nations on one planet under the sun. The same needs are shared. Polarized extremes have 90 per cent of common views. How we get there is the chasm. Focus on how to help. Do not dwell on hurt. Focus on the positives. Refuse anger and arguments. Shift from self-center to love-center.

Remember the quote from Yoda in "Star Wars:" "Do or do not. There is no try." Create the world we want to live in. Serve our loved ones. Help our friends and neighbors. Help those who will not be helped. Walk in love with everyone encountered. Provide for spiritual needs and remember the physical needs. Attitudes must be consistent with action. Be merciful to friends and enemies. Create peace. Love as God loves. Forgive as God forgives. Walking will not bring perfection. Journey toward that perfection. Be people of God.

Freed from anger, we begin to transform the fire of anger into the fire of love. Love makes us conscious that we change and will always be in a place of change. Love keeps us accepting and in touch with our shadow.

No person is completely blind. Carry your light. Walk a million miles with a ten-foot light. Walk humbly. Be a bridge for joy. Wade deep in compassion.

The road that leads us to becoming our authentic selves converges with the road which guides on toward the mystery of God. The better we know ourselves, the more we know God.

Life is a mystery to be lived. Light arriving in darkness is a small miracle. Having expectations does not give control over what actually happens. In the winter season, we acknowledge the presence of mystery.

Hopes are disappointed. Faith in goodness may get shaken.

Imagine a small miracle is seeking you out. A small win brings hope. Give thanks. Small miracles, not big wins, will find us.

Sensitivity for times God touches us, assures us of the love. We are never alone. Recognize those gentle touches. Remember the joys. Read John 16:22. Rest knowing that life is in God's care.

God's love for life is better than ours. We are designed to be joyful and delightful from our spiritual roots, for the simple reason that God is that way and we imitate God.

Our earth journey enables us to discern what is the will of God. The whispering wisdom that begins from within is the prompting of the Spirit.

Our earth journey is not where the pathway is easy and straight, but the road is full of twists and turns and unexpected surprises. When we become stuck, we can become intimate in prayer to help tap the stillness within.

Cling to hope. See beyond the seen to the unseen. The unseen is far more glorious that what can be seen on earth.

Shades of Joy in a Nursing Home

In retirement I have found joy for myself and those who live in nursing homes. Ministry to nursing homes, jails and prisons, hospices, and places that get little attention are harbingers of heaven. Sharing joy in these places creates experiences for elderly persons to provide meaningful everyday life.

Joy in the Seasons of Life

In a class at Midwestern Baptist Theological Seminary on pastoral care, students were introduced to the health theory of *autogenesis*, which indicates that a positive view of life positively influences an individual's health and well-being. The concept includes the perception that the world is comprehensible, meaningful, and manageable. Dr. Richard Day ringer was professor for this learning. Nursing homes are where *salutogenesis* is practiced.

The common thought was to accept the need to express needs for positive relationships, happiness, and meaning in life. People living satisfactorily in engage in daily activities. They feel valuable to others. They are free to make decisions. They experience small glimpses of the world outside. Some attend theater, concerts, restaurants, have visitors, and encouragement to accept one's way of life as it is.

Positive relations are associated with relationships to caring and loving family members and friends and being cared for by positive healthcare personnel. Residents want to tell their stories. Some have deep living insights and interesting experiences. Listening to these stories are valued in sharing the warm, long remembered thinking with feelings from childhood and special occasions.

People in every season seek joy. These feelings get farther away from us as we grow older. Joy is a love of life in its deepest form. It is not an emotion that declares everything in life is exactly how we want it in any particular season.

In all seasons and in all places, joy is the fruit of appreciation.

Joy in the Heart of a Prisoner

Paul's writing while in prison was tinged with joy. The Prison Epistles offer hope. The United States has more people housed in prison than any other nation. Some find joy in second chances. Life is simple in prison. I have been privileged to share the joy of the Lord in more than 150 prisons and jails. Every minister has an obligation to share with people imprisoned. Some reflect overflowing joy that puts smiles on faces.

Birds out early in the morning chirp at each other. Raindrops coming down make for new perspectives. Walking outside the cell at sunset brings quiet joy. Those who choose joy join with others and encourage them in their journeys to faith. A pastor can be a mentor as visiting, praying, and laughing bring encouragement and hope.

During a trip to Huntsville, Texas, I preached to prisoners in the state prison. I interviewed some of them for a story for Baptist Press when I wrote feature articles for the Sunday School Board. The prison officers allowed me to give an invitation to choose the joy of Christ, most raised a hand. Perhaps this was part of their redemptive journey.

Communion with God brings joy despite the circumstances. Intimate contact with God gives hope. When we ask what they find joy, they remind me and themselves of the difficulties Jesus endured including prison and execution. Believing in everlasting life brings pure joy. God loves those who live in prison or any institution unconditionally. Read John 3:16. In thankfulness for that infinite love, our souls always dance for joy.

Ministry in special institutions must involve being present, being thankful, listening to stories, and giving yourself permission to feel. People use much energy by worrying about the past or fearing the uncertainty of the future. Ask them what they are grateful for. Help them focus on these things. No human can focus on misery and at the same moment have a heart full of joy. Connection to your heart and soul is critical for joy. When the culture we create or the environment in which we live is caring, compassionate, and fun, and full of honest belonging, there we find joy. Life is not just about feeling good. Life is about being good at feeling. It is meaningful to feel all kinds of emotions during the never experienced, and to ask for help and support.

"A million little things make a difference." We must never forget to be grateful for the little moments that are extraordinary. Watch the seasons change. Await winter with hope. Enjoy the phone calls and notes from family and friends. Enjoy eating. As you wake up, anticipate what the day will provide. Choosing to wear favorite colors on a rainy day makes us feel better.

Leaving the home with a smile will get you smiles back. Place a vase of flowers in your kitchen. Little things cause you to enjoy life. These brief moments are celebrated. Reward yourself with a little present.

Laura King, professor of psychology at the University of Missouri in Columbia, led a team in research with the question, "The Benefits of Frequent Positive Affect: Does Happiness Lead to Success?"

This study covered more than a thousand pages. The research showed that happy people are successful. Positive affect engenders success. The hallmark of well-being causes desirable characteristics. The thesis is that the alternate causal pathway that people are likely to acquire favorable circumstances. This alternative and persuasive perspective of the role of positive affect as a mediator of happiness-success relation by broadening one's cognitive repertoire. This allows an accrual of resources for learning new skills.

This extensive research showed the key to success is a happy affect and not a happy genetic predisposition. "Peoples' current moods mediate the effects of chronic happiness on behavior." (Laura King, "The Benefits of Frequent Positive Affect: Does Happiness Lead to Success?" *Emotion*, spring 2009, pages 801-817, 843-996.)

The research concluded that evidence of a variety of outcomes will be needed to answer the question of how these "goods of life" relate to and promote each other. Secular and spiritual resources give assurance in our journeys.

This book contains stories from my journeys. As part of my calling to share my joy is that my discoveries will encourage you. I have struggled to integrate every awareness into my life. I admit I have erred and reverted to former patterns of thinking.

I have traveled the world sharing joy. Beginning again is possible because life is possible. Life contains sobering realities. We want to repair past relationships. Either the others are not willing or died. They could have moved on. I have developed deep compassion for each soul struggling with the realities in joyful moments.

During my four years as pastor of Faith Baptist Church in Nebraska City, I shared the same material on prayer that I shared with many groups on retreats. Some shared what had happened to them through prayer. One had lost his most valuable person in his life, his mother. His father died one day at the very hour he released him to God. Crying tears from guilt, he thought his prayer caused her to die. He related that his dad was a fine Christian. I assured him that giving him over to God did not cause the death. He was being prepared for the loss that was the will of God. Naturally, humans cling to the thought that it will be better to stay on earth than to go to an unknown heavenly home.

Separating bodies for souls was not the original plan. Turning loss into gain, our hearts are lifted to that glorious place of eternal joy.

As I conclude this book, I use the quote, "Don't postpone joy," as inspiration. These words stimulate me as I grasp hold of joy.

Too often we postpone joy. We wait until we graduate. We wait until we get a job. We wait until we are married. We wait until we retire. "Carpe diem" is another term for "don't postpone joy."

How we start sets the tone for the whole experience. Emotion colors perspective. Strengthened by joy, we notice surroundings that sustain.

Waking up on the wrong side of the bed, we can jumpstart a downward spiral. Joyful starts increase our awareness. We are more resilient.

The days filled with joy cause heaven's harbinger more than the eye can imagine. As this writing comes to a close, ask God to give you a proper perspective as we view others with God's eyes. Stand on tiptoes. Look beyond the bulkhead of obstacles. Fix the eyes on joy. Life on earth is temporary. Read II Corinthians 4:17. Focus on eternal life. Approach the hurt on this side of life with joy waiting. Attain the perspective of joy. Travel the detours by seeing what God sees.

Focus on Jesus. Follow his ways. Look at troubles as building blocks. Constructive results come from destructive forces. God directs us in a consistency of joy.

Look past the unpleasantness to find joy. Rocks in our path cannot keep us from joy. Remember earthly life is temporal. See rocks as building blocks. Step on the stones of confidence. They lead to eternal joy. Live life with pride. Stick with what is important. Being busy and being productive are not the same. Make a difference. Hug the hopeless. Comfort the grievers. Laugh with the sad.

Moaning is a trap. Groaning and whining are more traps. Grasp courage. Hold on with both hands. Fixing everything and everyone is an illusion. Entangling with that thought is a web of frustration, confusion, and stress. Stress is a mess. Go to a quiet place. Refocus. Let God deal with it. All pieces of the puzzle are in God's control. Leave the pieces where they are. Walk out of dark places knowing the puzzle will not be solved by us. Close the door. Walk into the light. Be something for someone. Care. Listen. Be kind. Do only what we have power to do.

Winter is now for many. The final days are near. Little blessings along the journey keep us from letting something that does not matter lose out to something that really matters. Taste the joy of each day. Walk each other home.

When I was in college, I had headaches. I found much difficulty in making out the words on the white board in front of the room. I made an appointment with an optometrist to check my eyes. He said that I needed glasses.

Once I began wearing them, my head aches left. The blurry vision swiftly disappeared. Recently, my eyes troubled me again. The eye specialists suggested that harm resulted from time spent on my laptop screen each day as an author. I received a new set of glasses to be worn only in front of the computer. I wear mid-distance glasses in my home office. I wear regular glasses the rest of the time.

We look at our lives through the wrong lens. What we see is blurry. Using the lens that God uses, we view ordinary life in a clearer manner. Our purpose on earth is made clear. God has perfect vision. We see God changing lives for eternity. We must slow down and adopt God's perspective.

Enjoy peace and quiet in your home. Most people can't do it. Noise rules. Think about it. In my travels, I observe people just surviving. They hang on. They get by. There is little enthusiasm for life. Parents, teachers, people everywhere ask, "What do you want to do when you grow up?" Better to say, "Who is God inviting me to become?" Perspective changes. God's dreams of more than you can imagine. I love to preach. An hour goes like five minutes. Time passes. I never notice. I live in joy.

Walking each other home from the expectation of others to the true self helps us be what God created us all to become. Discover your unique abilities. Feeling at home as your true self where we are comes in a joy. This is worth more than all the treasure on earth. Questing for worldly success never brings peace. Being authentic is being faithful to ourselves in God's joy.

Life is about love. Love doing what you do. Being true is love. Find what you love. Do it.

Be courageous. Create silence. Traveling to other places, changing jobs, changing houses, a new car, a new lover will not help. Searching is real and imaginary. We have imperfections. Accept your outward looks, the things we are not talented to do. Truth lived brings wisdom. God can see the plight of the mistreated, the oppressed, the marginalized as colossal and chronic. Reaching out to the least of these, we do not do it unnoticed.

A new year, 2022, is just around the corner. Putting life on hold is easy. We deserve time to loosen up the reins and enjoy festive December. Prepare to get 2022 off to a flying start.

Buy a new journal and plot your goals and plans. Opening up a journal is special. Write the social commitments, the places you can share your gifts. After Christmas, declutter your things and give them to people in need. Empty the wardrobe. Clean out drawers. Free the physical space in your home. Writers and ministers accumulate books. Give them away.

Reflect on the year gone. Compose a gratitude list. Writing words of thanksgiving will help stay rooted in the positives. Appreciation is the heart of joy.

Joy in Death

Emily Dickinson's poem, "Joy in Death," gave me a perspective on death. She wrote, "If toiling bell I ask the cause. A soul has gone to God. I'm answered in a lonesome tone; Is heaven then so sad. That bells should joyfully ring to tell a soul had gone to heaven, would seem to me the proper way good news should be given."

Her words focus on death not being a time of negative mourning. Celebrating the joy of going to heaven is beyond imagination. Death is not desolate and dark. Death is joy. "A soul has gone to God." Dickinson challenges, "Is death so bad?"

Dickinson begins with hearing a "tolling bell." She assures feeling as she writes, "That death now has bells should joyful ring to tell." The upbeat thought is that "a soul has gone on to heaven." Joy surrounds us because our loved ones are in "a better place."

The poem is straight forward. Misinterpreting or being confused are not possible. Heaven is happy and God and angels rejoice. "A soul has gone to heaven." My brother David suffered for years. He deserved rewards in heaven.

We should be joyful. It is difficult. We will never again be in their presence as long as we live. We shall never hear their voice until we too are released to heaven.

Life is full of separations. Feeling alone, abandoned, and forsaken whether unavoidable or deliberate as we hit bottom. The first day of kindergarten and going off to college with new clothes, eyes shining, we shed tears.

Death feels like a dream. We feel betrayed, angry, bitter, and lonely. We grieve for a lifetime. Grieving loss forces us to wrestle in spiritual and physical pain. Be open to glimpses of joy. Try something different. Do what you love. Make new traditions. Intentionally live for healing and acceptance. Experience joy in sounds, sights, and moments.

Walking with our families, we make banners in memory of loved ones. Memories can be expressed in art, poetry, or books. Be creative with each avenue for communication. Walking each other home helps us remember old memories. Forming new memories reveal another layer of life. Laugh with others. Shed tears. Shift perspectives. Prioritize anew. Walk each other home. See the long-range perspective. Joy is waiting. Use God's telescope. The best is yet to come.

When I preached a summer series on heaven, my church board approved. Together we thought it was inconceivable that a church creating an atmosphere for joy needed sermons on the ultimate destination. Read I Thessalonians 4:13.

Heaven is God's central dwelling place. The exact location of heaven is unknown. Heaven is our home in transition between the earthly journey and eternal resurrection life. The heavenly home is far better than earth, away from the direct presence of God.

Believing in eternal life, we will have a resurrected life. Our earthly journey matters. Informed perspective helps us to know that we will never reach peaks of full perfect development.

The best is yet to come.

I do not know how much string is left on my ball of twine. None of us know how much longer we have to live. I would rather make my days count than adding the days left on earth. I want to experience as much of God and family and friends as I can. Life is too short for each one. Enjoy it.

Prayer for Times of Not Feeling Joyful

Source of Joy, I know that with joy we have an eternal hope. This day I feel empty of joy. I sense the joylessness and I can't find how to sort it out.

Lord God, in bitterness and confusion, I beg to be filled. I want the joy found through Jesus. With no deserving of love and forgiveness, I give myself to be transformed with the joy of salvation.

Fill me with the joy of grace. Pour the Lord's strength into all who thrive with its power. Carry me I pray. Please place your arms around me. Without Your joy, I am lost.

Overflow me with that joy for all seasons. Be intimate with me as joy is known despite how I may feel. In Jesus' name. Amen.

Practical Applications

Develop your personal plan for experiencing joy when the season is a tough one. Establish a joy instinct strategy for creating an environment where joy will happen.

Exhaust your list of things you are thankful for in every season. Be the most grateful version of yourself. Be lavish with your list.

Make the following declaration: "I declare that from this day forward, I will walk toward joy. I will never walk away."

Think about a character trait that you admire in someone else. Embrace that trait into your own life.

Make the following declaration: "I declare today that I shall express joy regardless of how I feel."

Don't postpone joy. Embrace your real true self. Joy comes to you as you live as your wonderful self.

Share joy in this world that is constipated by its own superficiality. Life's difficulties allow us to break through to a deeper eternal joy within. Write a bucket list of upcoming opportunities. Joy is a continuing process The journey is muffled. Sometime it is detoured.

I hope you have enjoyed *Joy in All Seasons: Walking Each Other Home to God* It has been a joy and privilege to write for you. May God bless you with a prayerful spirit of joy as walk each other home.

Bibliography

Anderson, Neil T., Zuehlke, Terry. *Christ-Centered Therapy: The Practical Integration of Theology and Psychology*. Grand Rapids: Zondervan Publishing House, 2000.

Bertagnolli, O. T. and Rakham, John. *Creativity in the Writing Process*. New York: Wiley, 1982.

Bjork, Steven, Lindkvist,V., Edvardsson, David, "Exploring Resident: Thriving in Relation to Nursing Home Environment," Oslo: Wiley Library, 2018, *Advance Nur*sing, 74:2820-30.

Blanding, Michael, "Shot in the Arm," *Vanderbilt Magazine*, 102, (2) spring 2021, pp. 32-37.

Bradburn, N.M. *The Structure of Psychological Being*. Chicago: Alpine Press, 1969.

Brady, E. M. and Sky, H. Z., "Journal Writing Among Older Learners," *Educational Gerontology*, 29, 151-163, 2009.

Brice, Peter. *On the Edge: Wrestling with God in Depression*. Norwich, England: Millstream Press, 1995.

Brooks, David. *The Second Mountain: The Quest for a Moral Life*. New York: Random House, 2020.

Carter, Michael, "Trust, Power, and Vulnerability: A Discourse on Helping in Nursing Homes," *Clinical Nursing in North America*, 2009, 44, 393-405.

Cheever, John. *The Journals of John Cheever*. New York: Ballantine, 1999.

Chopra, Deepak. *Ageless Body, Timeless Mind*. New York: Harmony 1993.

Christenson, Evelyn. *Changing Your Life through the Power of Prayer*. New York: Inspirational Press, 1980.

Cole, Thomas. *The Journey of Life: A Cultural History of Aging in America*. Cambridge: Cambridge University Press, 1992.

Downs, Hugh. *Fifty to Forever*. Nashville: Thomas Nelson, 1994.

Dunne, John. *A Search for God in Time and Memory*. New York: Macmillan, 1996.

Elbow, Paul. *Writing without Teachers*. Oxford: Oxford University Press, 1998.

Emmons, R.A. "Joy Is a Distinct Positive Emotion: Assessment of Joy and Relationship to Gratitude and Well-Being," *The Journal of Positive Psychology*, 13 (5), 522-539, 2018.

Farber, David J., "Written Communication in Psychiatry," *Psychiatry*, 16, 365-379, 1953.

Farley, J.W., "Interactive Writing and Gifted Children: Communication Through Literary Art," *Journal for the Education of the Gifted*, 10, 99-111, 1999.

Farrar, Steve. *Family Survival in the American Jungle*. Portland: Multnomah Press, 1991.

Fox, Matthew. *Sheer Joy: Conversations with Thomas Aquinas*. New York: Harper/Collins, 1992.

Fredrickson, B. L., "What Good Are Positive Emotions?" *Review of General Psychology*, 2, 300-320, 1998.

Fuchel, John C., "Writing Poetry Enhances the Psychotherapeutic Process: Observation and Examples," *The Arts in Psychotherapy*, 122, 89-103, 1985.

Gillispie, Carl, "Recovery Poetic 101: The Use of Collaborative Poetry in a Dual-Diagnosis Drug and Alcohol Treatment Program, *Journal of Poetry Therapy*, 15 (2), 83-92, 2001.

Gire, James, "How Death Imitates Life: Cultural Influences on Conception of Death and Dying," *Psychology and Culture*, 6 (2), 2014.

Goldberg, Kenneth. *How Men Can Live as Long as Women*. New York: Summit Books, 206.Gordon, R.D., Dimensions of Peak Communication Experiences, *Psychological Reports*, 57, 824-829, 1989.

Gore, Amanda. *The Gospel of Joy*. Chatswood, Australia: Head2Heart Books, 2020.

Haugan, G., "Meaning-in-Life in Nursing Home Patients: A Valuable Approach for Enhancing Psychological and Physical Well-Being," *Journal of Clinical Nursing*, 2014, 23: 1830-1854.

Hollis, James. *Finding Meaning in the Second Half of Life*. New York: Gotham, 2006.Hontz, Marilyn. *Listening for God: How an Ordinary Person Can Learn to Hear God*. Wheaton: Tyndale Press, 2004.

Jacobsen, Wayne. *In Season*. Newbury Park, California: Trail View Media, 2020.

Jung, Karl. "The Stages of Life," *Collected Works of Karl Jung*. Princeton: Princeton University Press, vol. 8, pp. 398-399.

Killinger, John. *The Gospel of Contagious Joy: A Devotional Guide to Luke*. Waco, Texas: Word Books, 1980.

King, Laura, "The Benefits of Frequent Positive Affect: Does Happiness Lead to Success?"

King, L.A. and Broyles, S.J., "Wishes, Gender, Personality, and Well-Being," *Journal of Personality*, 65, 49-76, 1997.

Kinghorn, Kenneth. *Discovering Your Spiritual Gifts*. Grand Rapids: Zondevan, 2002.

Kinlaw, Dennis. *Coaching for Commitment*. San Francisco: Jossey-Bass, 2009.

Kirkland, Richard, "Why We Will Longer . . . and What It Will Mean," *Fortune*, February 21, 1994, pp. 66-86.

Kolata, Gina, "Study Challenges Longevity Theory," *New York Times*, October 16, 1992.

Knight, Walker. *Knight's Treasury of Illustrations*. Grand Rapids: Eerdman Publishing House, 1963.

Lahr, John. "Dead Souls," *The New Yorker*, May 9, 1996, pp. 93-98.

Lama, Dalai and Tutu, Desmond. *The Book of Joy*. New York: Random House, 2016.

Lebo, David. "Some Factors Said to Make for Happiness in Old Age," *Journal of Clinical Psychology*, 9, 385-387, 1998.

Lewis, C.S. The *Weight of Glory*. New York: Harper, 1976.

Lyubomirsky, Sonya. "Why Are Some People Happier Than Others?" *American Psychologist, 56, 239-249, 1997*.

McMinn, Mark. *Psychology, Theology, and Spirituality in Christian Counseling*. Wheaton: Tyndale House, 1996

McGrath, Alister. *The Journey*. New York: Doubleday, 2000.

McReynolds, James. *Alcoholism: America's Number One Drug Problem*. Nashville: Broadman Press, 1975.

McReynolds, James. *Dancing with God: A Theology of Joy*. Cleveland, Tennessee: Parson's Porch Books, 2016.

McReynolds, James. *Joy Comes in the Mourning: Love Is Forever*. Cleveland, Tennessee: Parson's Porch Books, 2020.

McReynolds, James. *Spirit of Joy Church*. Cleveland, Tennessee: Parson's Porch Press, 2019.

McReynolds, James. *The Joy of Prayer: The Way to Intimacy with God*. Cleveland, Tennessee: Parson's Porch Books, 2017.

McReynolds, James. *The Joy of Preaching: Encountering Jesus Through the Word of God*. Cleveland, Tennessee: Parson's Porch Books, 2013.

McReynolds, James. *The Joy of the Kingdom: Envisioning the Great Commission*. Cleveland, Tennessee: Parson's Porch Books, 2020.

McReynolds, James. *The Silence of the Church: The Spiritual Struggle with Sexuality*. Cleveland, Tennessee: Parson's Porch Books, 2017.

McReynolds, James. *The Spirituality of Joy*. Cleveland, Tennessee: Parson's Porch Books, 2011.

McReynolds, James. *Walking in the Garden with God*. Cleveland, Tennessee: Parson's Porch Books, 2021

Merton, Thomas. The Seven Storey Mountain. New York: Harcount Books, 1976.

Moore, Thomas. *Care of the Soul.* New York: Harper and Collins, 1992.

Moyers, Bill. *Healing and the Mind.* New York: Doubleday, 1996.

Nouwen, Henri. *The Inner Voice of Love.* New York: Image Books, 1999.

Ortberg, John. *If You Want to Walk on Water, You've Got to Get Out of the Boat.* Grand Rapids: Zondervan, 2002.

Pettit, J. W., Gencoz, F. E., and Joiner, T.E., "Are Happy People Healthier: The Specific Role of Positive Affect in Predicting Self-Reported Health Symptoms, *Journal of Research in Personality*, 35, 521-536, 2006.

Pippert, Rebecca. *Out of the Salt-Shaker and into the World.* Downer's Grove: Inter/varsity Press, 1999.

Riddick, C.C. "Life Satisfaction Determinants of Older Males and Females," *Leisure Sciences*, 7, 47-63, 1985.

Ripple, Paula. *Called to Be Friends.* Notre Dame: Ave Maria Press, 1999.

Rupp, Joyce. *Inviting God In: Scriptural Reflections and Prayers Throughout the Year.* Notre Dame, Indiana: Ave Maria Press, 2001.

Ryff, C.D., "Happiness Is Everything, or Is It? Explorations in the Meaning of Psychological Well-Being," *Journal of Personality and Social Psychology*, 57, 1069-1081, 1990.

Ryff, C.D., "The Contours of Positive Human Health," *Psychological Inquiry*, 9, 1-28, 1998.

Samuels, Mike and Nancy. *Seeing with the Mind's Eye*. New York: Random House, 1985.

Sheehy, Gail. *New Passages: Mapping Your Life Across Time*. Thorndike, Maine: G.K. Hall and Company, 1995.

Sheehy, Gail. *Passages*. New York: Random House, 1992.

Sheehy, Gail. *The Silent Passage*. New York: Random House, 1992.

Spurgeon, Charles H. *Beside Still Waters*. Nashville: Thomas Nelson Books, 1999.

Stack, Steve, and Eshleman, J.R., "Marital Status and Happiness: A Nation Study," *Journal of Marriage and Family Therapy*, 60, 527-536, 1998.

Stott, John. *Christian Basics: A Handbook of Beginnings, Beliefs, and Behaviors*. Grand Rapids, 2005.

Tannen, Deborah. *You Just Don't Understand*. New York: Morrow, 1997.

Taylor, Kenneth. *My Life: A Guided Tour*. Wheaton: Tyndale House, 2000.

Tournier, Paul. *The Seasons of Life*. Richmond, Virginia: John Knox Press, 1963.

Updike, John. *The Afterlife*. New York: Knopf, 1996.

Van Cappellen, Peter. "Rethinking Self-Transcendent Positive Emotions and Religion: Insights from Psychological and Biblical Research," *Psychology of Religion and Spirituality*, 9 (3), 254-265, 2017.

Volf, Miroslav, "Joy Is Not Merely External," *Joy and Flourishing*. Minneapolis: Fortress Press, 2015.

Watkins, P.C. "Joy Is a Distinct Positive Emotion: Assessment of Joy in Relationship to Gratitude," lecture, Yale University Center for Faith and Culture, New Haven, summer 2009.

Watson, David, "Intra-Individual and Inter-Individual Analyses of Positive and Negative Affect: Their Relation to Health Complaints, Stress, and Daily Activities, *Journal of Personality and Social Psychology*, 54, 1020-1044, 1988.

Weiss, Rick, "A Shot at Youth," *Health*, November-December 1993, pp. 38-49.

Whyte, David. *Joy Is the Meeting Place*. Langley, Washington: Many Rivers Press, 2013.

Wills, Dick. *Waking to God's Dream*. Nashville: Abingdon Press, 1999.

Wilson, William, "Correlates of Avowed Happiness," *Psychological Bulletin*, 67, 294-306, 1997.

Wright, N.T. *Some New Testament Perspectives on Joy and Flourishing*. Minneapolis: Fortress Press, 2015.Zdenek, Marilee. Splinters in My Pride. Waco, Texas: Word Publishing 1979.

Acknowledgements

I am grateful to John Killinger, David Tullock, Bryan Baker, David Clark, James Andrews, Jillian Baker, Cameryn and McKenzie Richardson, Michael Njus, members of Elmwood Christian, James Gordon, Ethan Coffin, Rick and Carmen Richardson, A. J. Bieber, and thoughtful comments made in the early stages of this writing.

Various support groups gave me the opportunity to share my ideas. I am grateful for those who attended my workshops and vision quests in churches and schools.

I thank my daughter Linda McReynolds, who encouraged her dad with reflections that have given the final forms of my books.

Books that offered me a lifeline when I was stuck are listed in the bibliography. I owe a debt to each of them. I have attributed key ideas to the authors within the text.

I owe so much to my teachers in the host of schools where I have gained new insight. My graduate courses in psychology introduced me to cognitive therapy. My instructors at the Graduate Theological Foundation in Notre Dame, Indiana introduced the technique of talking back to feelings that distressed me.

Special thanks to Dr. David Tullock, who has found his niche as the president and publisher of Parson's Porch Books. His group has published at least a third of my books on aspects of joy.

Thanks to my expanding prayer group for hitting their knees for my ministries. I am grateful for every member of my family.

Most of all, my greatest debt is to my wife Laurel for suggestions that made a critical difference in several passages. Her emotional and spiritual support made the hours of writing this book possible.

Thanks to the thousands of people that I interviewed in the past 50 years and found them unique and inspirational. I have learned that joy is not just an academic or church or Christmas topic, but that joy must be experienced in the context of community perception, biblical insight, tolerance, and courage. I would never have chosen to follow God's mysterious calling without those that I encountered on my life journey. Without their insight and direction, this book would never have been written.

Hundreds of people impacted this volume. Many made suggestions. Encouragers cheered me on. Others influenced my life and ministry. I thank God for placing each one in my path.

About the Author

James McReynolds has spoken on joy more than anyone in history. He has a comprehensive ministry approach that he has researched, designed, created, experienced, and shared.

With his quests for joy, he discusses the psychology and spirituality of joy. He earned a doctorate in preaching, worship, and literature. Jim earned a degree in journalism from the University of Missouri. He has degrees in English literature, psychology, religious education, and thousands of hours of continuing education.

Mass media communication includes writing thousands of news articles for Baptist Press and numerous denominational magazines, weekly newspaper columns, countless books, and radio and television including "Serendipity: A Religious Television Outreach," and using TV and radio and newspapers to promote the 22 programs of the Sunday School Board of the largest Protestant denomination in the United States.

As the minister of joy to the world, he helps people of faith and no faith understand the vocation to live joyfully. In this volume, Jim goes beyond material covered in his other books to stress faith involved in relating to God as we relate to personal joy. Joy is the lasting awareness of God's joy in us. The world will not and cannot give.

His faith commitment to God is to go where joylessness makes some miserable. Dr. McReynolds has preached and shared joy in all 49 nations in the continent of Africa, where in some countries the age of 30 is considered the life expectancy. Black lives have always mattered to Jim. And all lives matter to God. Contact Information to Reach the Minister of Joy to the world. Contact James McReynolds for a conference, retreat, radio-TV interview, or a group training at 402-994-2370, joyminister@windstream.net internet or letter to 320 North 4th Street, Elmwood, Nebraska 68349.